PARABLES FOR PREACHERS

Parables for Preachers
The Gospel of Mark
YEAR B

Barbara E. Reid, O.P.

A Liturgical Press Book

THE LITURGICAL PRESS
Collegeville, Minnesota

1   2   3   4   5   6   7   8

Library of Congress Cataloging-in-Publication Data

Reid, Barbara E.
    Parables for preachers / Barbara E. Reid.
      p. c.m.
    Includes bibliographical references.
    Contents: — [2] Year B. The Gospel of Mark.
    ISBN 0-8146-2551-7 (v. 2 : alk. paper)
    1. Jesus Christ—Parables—Homiletical use. 2. Bible. N.T. Mark—Criticism, interpretation, etc. 3. Bible. N.T. Mark—Homiletical use. 4. Lectionary preaching—Catholic Church.
BT375.2.R45   1999
226.8'06—dc21   99-28090
                                             CIP

In gratitude to those preachers,
especially my Dominican sisters,
whose telling of the Gospel story
has fed and converted me.

Contents

Marcan Parables in the Lectionary

SUNDAY LECTIONARY:

Five Marcan passages with parables are assigned to the Sunday lectionary.

Four are also assigned to a weekday, as follows:

Mark 2:18-22: Eighth Sunday of Ordinary Time
                     Monday, Week 2 of Ordinary Time

Mark 3:20-35: Tenth Sunday of Ordinary Time
                     Monday, Week 3 of Ordinary Time (Mark 3:22-30)

Mark 4:26-34: Eleventh Sunday of Ordinary Time
                     Friday, Week 3 of Ordinary Time

Mark 7:1-8, 14-15, 21-23. Twenty-second Sunday of
                     Ordinary Time
                     Wednesday Week 5 of Ordinary Time
                     (Mark 7:14-23)

Mark 13:24-32: Thirty-third Sunday of Ordinary Time

WEEKDAY LECTIONARY:

The following Marcan parables appear only in the weekday lectionary:

Mark 4:1-20: Wednesday, Week 3 of Ordinary Time

Mark 4:21-25: Thursday, Week 3 of Ordinary Time

Mark 12:1-12: Monday, Week 9 of Ordinary Time

Abbreviations

AB	Anchor Bible
ABD	*Anchor Bible Dictionary* ed. David N. Freedman
ABRL	Anchor Bible Reference Library
B.C.E.	Before the Christian Era
BETL	Bibliotheca ephimeridum theologicarum lovaniensium
Bib	*Biblica*
BibInt	*Biblical Interpretation*
BibSac	*Bibliotheca Sacra*
BR	*Biblical Research*
BTB	*Biblical Theology Bulletin*
BullBibRes	*Bulletin for Biblical Research*
C.E.	Christian Era
CBQ	*Catholic Biblical Quarterly*
CBQMS	CBQ Monograph Series
EB	Études Bibliques
EspVie	*Esprit et Vie*
ExpTim	*Expository Times*
GNS	Good News Studies Series
ICC	International Critical Commentary
Int	*Interpretation*
JBL	*Journal of Biblical Literature*
JR	*Journal of Religion*
JSJ	*Journal for the Study of Judaism*
JSNT	*Journal for the Study of the New Testament*

JSNTSup	JSNT Supplement Series
JSOT	*Journal for the Study of the Old Testament*
JTS	*Journal of Theological Studies*
LXX	Septuagint (Greek Translation of the Hebrew OT)
MillStud	*Milltown Studies*
NAB	*New American Bible*
NJB	*New Jerusalem Bible*
NJBC	*New Jerome Biblical Commentary* (Ed. R. E. Brown *et al.*)
NovT	*Novum Testamentum*
NRSV	*New Revised Standard Version*
NT	New Testament
NTMS	New Testament Message Series
NTS	*New Testament Studies*
OT	Old Testament
RB	*Revue Biblique*
RevExp	*Review & Expositor*
RSR	*Religious Studies Review*
SBEC	Studies in the Bible and Early Christianity Series
SBL	Society of Biblical Literature
SBLDS	Society of Biblical Literature Dissertation Series
SBLMS	Society of Biblical Literature Monograph Series
ScEs	*Science et Esprit*
SJT	*Scottish Journal of Theology*
SNTSMS	Society for New Testament Studies Monograph Series
TBT	*The Bible Today*
WUNT	Wissenschaftliche Untersuchungen zum Neuen Testament
ZNW	*Zeitschrift für die neutestamentliche Wissenschaft*

Introduction

A disciple once complained,
  "You tell us stories,
  but you never reveal their meaning to us."
Said the master,
  "How would you like it if someone
  offered you fruit and masticated it
  before giving it to you?"[1]

In the Synoptic Gospels, Jesus rarely explains his parables.[2] They are meant to be wrestled with by each generation of hearers who allow themselves to be disturbed and challenged by Jesus' subversive stories. Yet Sunday after Sunday the preacher is asked to open up the meaning of parables to their congregations. How can a preacher avoid offering pre-masticated fruit? How can the one who opens up the Scriptures do so in a way that enhances the savory offerings therein without ruining the power of the story? How can a preacher offer fresh fare when the same parable appears time after time in the lectionary?

The first aim of this book is to aid preachers by bringing together current biblical research on the parables in the hope that it will open up new vistas of meaning for them and will spark their own creativity. Second, the book offers an understanding of how parables communicate, and invites the preacher to try out parabolic techniques of preaching. The

---

[1] Anthony de Mello, *The Song of the Bird* (Garden City, N.Y.: Doubleday, 1984) 1.

[2] The exceptions are the seed parable explained in Mark 4:13-20 and pars., the parable of the weeds explained in Matt 13:36-43, and the explanation of defilement from within in Mark 7:17-23. Most scholars believe these to be creations of the early Church and not from the lips of Jesus.

Synoptic Gospels show Jesus preaching primarily by means of parables, spoken and lived. A greater understanding of the dynamics and meaning of Jesus' parables in their original context can aid preachers today in creating the same effect in modern believers in a new context. This book is intended not only for preachers but for all who are interested in a deeper understanding of the parables, particularly teachers, catechists, liturgy planners, and members of groups for homily preparation, Bible study, or faith sharing.

PARABLES IN THE LECTIONARY

The term "parable" covers a wide range of figurative speech: similitudes, extended metaphors, symbolic expressions, exemplary and true-to-life stories. Included in this volume are all passages in the Gospel of Mark in which the term *parabolē* ("parable") occurs[3] as well as one story told in parabolic form (Mark 2:18-22) that Luke designates as a parable (Luke 5:36). There are other sayings and stories that could well be considered parabolic not included in this study. In one sense, the whole Gospel can be considered a parable. As John R. Donahue puts it, the parables "offer a Gospel in miniature and at the same time give shape, direction, and meaning to the Gospels in which they are found. To study the parables of the Gospels is to study the gospel in parable."[4]

Other volumes in this series treat the parables of Matthew (Lectionary Cycle A) and Luke (Lectionary Cycle C). Parables are noticeably absent from the Gospel of John. The fourth evangelist never uses the term *parabolē*, nor does he preserve any of Jesus' stories in the same parabolic form as do the Synoptic writers. Nonetheless symbolic speech abounds in the Fourth Gospel. The closest thing to a parable is found in chapter 10, where Jesus speaks of himself as the Good Shepherd and the gate for the sheep. And in John 10:6 Jesus' disciples have the same difficulty in understanding this "figure of

---

[3] The term *parabolē* occurs twelve times in the Gospel of Mark: 3:23; 4:2, 10, 11, 13, 30, 33, 34; 7:17; 12:1, 12; 13:28. It occurs sixteen times in Matthew, eighteen times in Luke, and twice in Hebrews.

[4] John R. Donahue, *The Gospel in Parable* (Philadelphia: Fortress, 1988) ix.

speech" (*paroimia*) as they do with the parables in Mark 4:10-12. The term *paroimia* occurs two more times in the Gospel of John (16:25, 29), where Jesus assures the disciples that a time will come when he will no longer speak in "figures" but plainly. This comes on the heels of the comparison of the disciples' anguish at Jesus' departure with that of a woman in labor. As she forgets her pain after her child is born, so will the disciples' grief turn into joy (16:21-24).

In the first chapter we explore the dynamics of Jesus' parables. Understanding how a parable "works" is the first step. Chapter 2 sketches contemporary trends in biblical interpretation of the parables. Next is an overview of the Gospel of Mark, its author, historical context, and major theological themes. The remaining chapters examine each of the parables of the Gospel of Mark in the order in which they appear in the lectionary for Year B. We will first treat the parables that appear in the Sunday lectionary, followed by those that appear only in the weekday lectionary. The concluding chapter and bibliography point toward further areas of study.

CHAPTER ONE

Preaching Parabolically

TO PREACH AS JESUS DID[1]

Jesus was not the first to preach in parables. There is a long tradition of such storytelling in the ancient world, not only by religious figures, but by rhetoricians, politicians, prophets, and philosophers as well. In the Hebrew Scriptures there are several examples of parables. In 2 Samuel 12:1-12, for example, the prophet Nathan tells King David a parable about a rich man who took a poor man's lone ewe lamb and made it into a meal for a visitor. The song of the vineyard in Isaiah 5:1-7 and the sayings about plowing and threshing in Isaiah 28:23-29 present agricultural metaphors not unlike those used by Jesus in his parables. The Jewish rabbis also spoke in parables.[2]

One result of parabolic preaching is that the storyteller allows the listener to back away from a sensitive topic and enter into a make-believe (but true-to-life) situation, where one can see more clearly what is right. Nathan successfully brought David to repentance for taking Uriah's wife when the king angrily pronounced sentence on the rich man of the parable. In the Synoptic Gospels we see Jesus using the same technique, for example, when addressing Simon the Pharisee in Luke 7:40-48; or when driving home his point to the Pharisees and scribes in Luke 15:1-32. Contemporary preachers can become more skilled in using

---

[1] An earlier version of this chapter, entitled "Preaching Justice Parabolically," appeared in *Emmanuel* 102/6 (1996) 342–47.

[2] On rabbinic connections with Jesus' parables see Philip L. Culbertson, *A Word Fitly Spoken* (Albany: State University of New York Press, 1995); Brad H. Young, *Jesus and His Jewish Parables. Rediscovering the Roots of Jesus' Teaching* (New York: Paulist, 1989); *The Parables. Jewish Tradition and Christian Interpretation* (Peabody: Hendrickson, 1998).

the same dynamics of storytelling as did Jesus, and thus engage their listeners more effectively with the Gospel message.

ENCOUNTER WITH THE HOLY

Before attempting to emulate Jesus' way of preaching, a preacher must know Jesus and his message first-hand. An effective preacher speaks from his or her personal and ongoing encounter with Christ in study, in prayer, in other people, and in all creation. Just as Jesus' constant communion with God[3] shaped his preaching, so must this be the foundation for the contemporary preacher. It is evident when a person speaks of the Holy whether they speak from their own experience or merely pass on what they have heard or studied. Intimate experience of the Divine in prayer is what energizes, sustains, and transforms the preacher. The inability to bring about deeply unitive experiences of prayer by one's own efforts keeps the preacher aware that these are gifts. So too is the ministry of preaching. It is God's word that a preacher speaks.

It is the joy of having experienced oneself as the object of God's love and delight that impels the contemplative preacher to share this message. There is the ever-present danger that the other demands of ministry erode the minister's time for prayer. Another pitfall is to let a striving for prayerfulness at all times take the place of specific time set aside for contemplative prayer. One who allows this to happen runs the risk of preaching a hollow word.

THE FAMILIAR RADICALLY TWISTED

In his parables, Jesus always began with the familiar. The images and situations he painted in his stories were from the fabric of daily life of his audience. He told how God is encountered in sowing and reaping (Mark 4:1-9), in weeding and harvesting (Matt 13:24-30), in baking bread (Matt 13:33), in searching for what is lost (Luke 15:1-32). In this way he would capture peoples' attention and draw them along with him to

---

[3] The Gospel of Luke has the most references to Jesus' habitual prayer: 3:21; 6:12; 9:18, 28; 11:1; 22:32, 41; 23:46. In the Gospel of Mark see 1:35; 6:46; 14:32, 35, 39.

the end of the story. In the same manner, an effective preacher today transforms the Gospel images and situations into ones that relate to the everyday world of those gathered. For example, the majority of the assembly will quickly tune out when the homily begins, "When I was in the seminary . . ." Or if the Gospel presumes rural, pre-industrial experiences when the gathered community is composed of urban professionals, the homilist will need to recontextualize the message for the contemporary situation.

In Jesus' parables no sphere of life is outside God's realm: the political, social, economic, ecclesial, and theological are all intertwined, as in the parables of the rich man and Lazarus (Luke 16:19-31); the rich fool (Luke 12:16-21); the dishonest steward (Luke 16:1-8); the parable of the great banquet (Matt 22:1-14; Luke 14:15-24); the Pharisee and the tax collector (Luke 18:9-14); the widow and the judge (Luke 18:1-8). Jesus' preaching brought a vision of all life as locus for the sacred; nothing is outside the realm of the holy. Likewise, a preacher today will help the assembly to see that holiness is not found by separating oneself from "the world," but is encountered in all reality. S/he will lead people to see God in the midst of the contradictions and the chaos, in the crucifying and dying, not only in the peacefulness and the rising to new life.

Jesus' parables do not stay on the level of the familiar. Always there is a catch. They were not pleasant stories that entertained people or that confirmed the status quo. They were startling and confusing, usually having an unexpected twist that left the hearers pondering what the story meant and what it demanded. As John Dominic Crossan puts it, "You can usually recognize a parable because your immediate reaction will be self-contradictory: 'I don't know what you mean by that story but I'm certain I don't like it.'"[4]

Jesus' parables are invitations to see the realm of God as God sees it and to act as Jesus acted. Such a vision demands profound changes in the way the hearer thinks about God and the realm of God, both as it can be in the here and now and in its future fullness. By shattering the structures of our accepted

---

[4] John Dominic Crossan, *The Dark Interval: Towards a Theology of Story* (Niles, Ill.: Argus Communications, 1975) 56.

world parables remove our defenses and make us vulnerable to God.[5] Preachers should be suspicious of interpretations that reinforce life as it is.[6] The Gospel is always about change. An effective preacher studies the text so as to understand what it originally meant and then tries to repeat that unsettling dynamic in their own preaching.

THE RIDDLE OF INTERPRETATION

One difficulty with Jesus' parables is that they are open-ended; Jesus rarely interpreted these stories for his disciples. For example, at the end of the story of the prodigal son (Luke 15:11-32), does the elder brother go in to the party after the father pleads with him? Or does he remain outside, angry and resentful? There lies the challenge. Jesus does not give the answer, but leaves it up to the hearer to determine the rest of the story. Over the ages each community of Christians has had to work out their responses to the challenges of Jesus' teaching; this task is no less incumbent upon believers today. Just as Jesus did not give the interpretation to his parables, neither do effective preachers provide pat answers.

Because they are told in figurative language, the parables are capable of conveying distinct messages to different people in diverse circumstances.[7] For instance, to a person in need of forgiveness, the parable in Luke 15:11-32 is the story of a lost son or daughter, who is invited to let him or herself be found by God and be lavished with love that cannot be earned. For a person in authority, the same story may serve as a call to emulate the character of the father who searches out ones who have embarked on a destructive path and runs to meet them and bring them back, at great personal cost. For persons who try always to be faithful to following God's ways, the story invites them to let go of joyless resentment and slavish attitudes in their service of God. The point of the story depends on one's point of entry and

[5] Ibid., 122.
[6] This is the function of myth rather than parable. See Crossan, *The Dark Interval*, 47–62.
[7] See Mary Ann Tolbert, *Perspectives on the Parables. An Approach to Multiple Interpretations* (Philadelphia: Fortress, 1979).

the character with whom one identifies. A preacher cannot be content with one stock interpretation, but must continually plumb the depths of the text for other possible meanings. On each occasion s/he must discern which of the many possible messages is the word that now needs be spoken.

BREVITY

The parables of Jesus are short and to the point. Some are only one line long. Like the Argentinian poet Jorge Luis Borges who laughed at those who wanted "to go on for five hundred pages developing an idea whose perfect oral expression is possible in a few minutes,"[8] Jesus knew the art of pithy expression. The brevity of the parables makes them easy to remember and enhances their ability to communicate forcefully. Likewise, when a preacher can convey his or her message briefly, there is a better chance that the word will be remembered and its transforming potential will be more fully released.

STANCE WITH THE MARGINAL

While multiple interpretations are possible, the preacher always tells the story slant, inviting the hearers to take a particular position in the narrative. Jesus often did this in telling his parables. And the stance to which he invites his hearers is with the marginal. For example, when addressing Pharisees and scribes that complained against him welcoming sinners and eating with them (Luke 15:1-2), Jesus asks them, "What man among you having a hundred sheep and losing one of them would not leave the ninety-nine in the desert and go after the lost one until he finds it?" (Luke 15:4).[9] Jesus has deliberately asked them to take the stance of the shepherd.

To understand the twist in this, it is important to know that although "shepherd" was used as an image for God (e.g.,

---

[8] John Dominic Crossan (*Cliffs of Fall. Paradox and Polyvalence in the Parables of Jesus* [New York: Seabury, 1980] 3) relays this quote from the Prologue of Jorge Luis Borges, *Ficciones* (New York: Grove, 1962).

[9] All biblical quotations, unless otherwise indicated, are taken from *New American Bible* with revised New Testament, 1986.

Psalm 23), and as a metaphor for religious leaders (e.g., Ezekiel 34), real shepherds in Jesus' day were disdained as dishonest and thieving. Jesus asked the Pharisees and scribes, religious leaders who thought themselves upright, to consider themselves as despised shepherds. The power of the story lies in the invitation to identify with people who are marginalized and to take their part. If that were not shocking enough, in the next parable (Luke 15:8-10), Jesus asks them to put themselves in the place of a woman who invests enormous energy to seek out a lost coin. The challenge to the religious leaders was not only to emulate shepherds and women who expend themselves greatly to bring back the lost, but also to be able to see a despised shepherd or an "inferior" woman as embodying God in the same way they imagined of themselves.

Jesus' parables proclaim that God is not neutral. Rather, God is always on the side of those who are poorest and most oppressed. Because of the inequities that exist, God must take their part in order to balance the scales.[10] One of the most crucial tasks of the preacher today, particularly in gatherings of those who are comfortable financially and socially, is to take up the perspective of those who are marginalized and invite the congregation to do the same. The point is not to make people feel guilty, but rather to move them to see from the perspective of those most disadvantaged and to ask then, what would love require of me? If one is not poor, then Christian discipleship demands solidarity with the poor, service to the needs of the least, and readiness to suffer persecution that follows from these actions.

A COMMUNAL ENDEAVOR

One of the more difficult aspects of preaching, especially in contemporary American culture, is to present gospel living as a communal endeavor, not a pursuit of individual salvation.[11]

---

[10] See, e.g., Clodovis Boff and Jorge Pixley (*The Bible, the Church, and the Poor* [Theology and Liberation Series; Maryknoll, N.Y.: Orbis, 1989]) who demonstrate how in every section of the Bible, God's concern is always for the poor.

[11] See further Edward J. Van Merrienboer, "Preaching the Social Gospel" in *In the Company of Preachers* (Ed. R. Siegfried and E. Ruane. Collegeville: The Liturgical Press, 1993) 176–90.

From its inception, the people of God is a community bound together by the covenant. But there is a further twist in the vision of community that Jesus' parables present. In the story of The Great Feast (Luke 14:15-24), for example, the people of God encompasses all—particularly the most despised and outcast. Or, consider Jesus' parable of the workers in the vineyard (Matt 20:1-16) for an entirely unsettling vision of a just community. The configuration is not that of each one pulling his or her own weight with appropriate compensation. Rather, the believing community is one in which each member has the means by which to subsist for the day, no matter what his or her contribution to the group.

A LIVED PARABLE

The ultimate aim of preaching is that the word be acted upon. The desired effect is that people's hearts be moved to praise of God that finds further expression in transformative action. Such a word gives hope and courage to those oppressed. It declares that injustice is not God's desire and it emboldens impoverished communities to act together for change. For those who are privileged, the preached word moves them not only to love and to stand with the wronged, but to act in solidarity with them to dismantle unjust structures. The power of Jesus' preaching came from his very life being a parable.[12] His paradoxical choice of death to bring life, of self-emptying to bring fullness for all, of humiliation and suffering to bring dignity and joy to the oppressed, proclaimed a radically different way to God. It was a life that issued an invitation to conversion and left people struggling to understand its meaning and demands. Effective preachers give such a parabolic witness in our day. No preaching takes root unless the life of the preacher is a living witness.[13] This witness, like the

---

[12] See Crossan, *The Dark Interval*, 123–28 on "The Parabler Becomes Parable" and John R. Donahue, "Jesus as the Parable of God in the Gospel of Mark," *Int* 32 (1978) 369–86.

[13] Pope Paul VI underscored this in his address to members of the *Consilium de Laicis* on October 2, 1974, when he said, "Modern man [sic] listens more willingly to witnesses than to teachers, and if he [sic] does listen to teachers, it is because they are witnesses" (*Evangelii Nuntiandi*, §21, 41).

parables, prompts all whose lives are touched by the preacher to ask, "What does this mean?" "What am I to do?" "What does this ask of me?" If the life of a preacher does not present a paradox, then the power of the Gospel s/he preaches is weakened.

Effective preachers are aware that they preach what their own lives proclaim imperfectly. The word takes root, though, when the preacher visibly joins in the struggle with the gathered community, together seeking to conform their lives ever more to that of Christ. Together they seek contemplative intimacy with God, engage in serious study of the word, both in the biblical text, and in their lived reality.

Such a preacher must be willing to be consumed by a passion for the gospel and its all-encompassing demands, willing even to risk rejection and opposition. The prophet Jeremiah, who tried to hold in the word, says it became "like fire burning in my heart" (Jer 20:9) and he could not resist speaking it forth. With such passion for the Gospel, a preacher becomes a sign of hope, not a prophet of doom. In parabolically proclaiming the vision of Jesus, it is not naive optimism that the preacher declares, nor a depressing guilt trip, but a word that galvanizes the community to conversion of heart and transformative action that is undergirded by profound love for all God's people.

CHAPTER TWO

Interpreting Parables

SPOILING THE PUNCHLINE

To have to interpret a parable is like having to explain a joke when someone misses the punchline. Yet, because of our familiarity with the parables, our lack of understanding of their rhetoric and of how Jesus' first audience would have reacted to his stories, we can miss the punchline of a parable. A critical step in the preparation for preaching a parable is serious biblical study that attempts to retrieve, as far as possible, what the story meant in its original telling. The preacher then attempts to re-effect such a dynamic in the contemporary context. Preaching that simply explains the original meaning to the assembly is instructional, but does not achieve its purpose.

DIFFICULTIES IN UNDERSTANDING THE PARABLES

In the Gospels, the disciples question Jesus about the parables because they do not understand (Mark 4:10-13 and pars.). The parables are far from simple stories that make Jesus' teaching easy to grasp. Although Jesus used familiar imagery, the stories remained enigmatic and confusing.[1] They are no less challenging to contemporary interpreters. Three factors contribute to our difficulty in understanding: the nature of the parables, the nature of the Gospels, and the nature of our sources of knowledge about the ancient world.

---

[1] Andrew Parker (*Painfully Clear. The Parables of Jesus* [Biblical Seminar 37; Sheffield: Sheffield Academic Press, 1996]) argues that Jesus' parables were not meant to be enigmatic. They were painfully clear and confrontational.

THE NATURE OF THE PARABLES

Parables, by their very nature, are puzzling. They are figurative speech, symbolic language, with more than one level of meaning.[2] The term "parable" *(parabolē* in Greek; *māshāl* in Hebrew) has a wide range of meanings. It can refer to a proverb, such as "physician cure yourself" (Luke 4:23). A wisdom saying or a riddle, such as, "Nothing that enters one from outside can defile that person; but the things that come out from within are what defile" (Mark 7:15) is dubbed a parable (Mark 7:17). A similitude, or a slightly developed comparison can be called a parable, as the lesson *(parabolē)* of the fig tree (Mark 13:28-29). The author of Hebrews twice uses the term in the sense of "symbol" (Heb 9:9; 11:19).

Gospel commentators often divide the parables of Jesus into three categories: similitude, parable, and exemplary story.[3] Similitudes are concise narratives that make a comparison between an aspect of God's realm and a typical or recurrent event in real life (e.g., seed growing in Mark 4:26-29; or losing a coin in Luke 15:8-10). Parables are usually longer and more detailed. They tell a story about a one-time fictitious, but true-to-life event, such as that of a widow who confronts an unjust judge (Luke 18:1-8) or a steward who faces dismissal (Luke 16:1-8). An exemplary story (e.g., the Good Samaritan in Luke 10:29-37) presents a specific example that illustrates a general principle. It differs from a similitude and a parable in that its comparison is between two things that are similar, not dissimilar.

Whichever form a parable takes, it is not an entertaining story that confirms the status quo. Its purpose is to persuade the hearer to adopt a particular view of God and life in God's realm. The aim of parables is to convert the hearer. They turn the world upside down by challenging presumptions, reversing expectations, and proposing a different view of life with God. Their open endings make it necessary for the hearers of every age to grapple with their implications.

---

[2] See John Dominic Crossan, *Cliffs of Fall. Paradox and Polyvalence in the Parables of Jesus* (New York: Seabury, 1980) 1–24 on Paradox and Metaphor; and 65–104 on Polyvalence and Play.

[3] E.g., M. Boucher, *The Parables* (NTM 7; Wilmington, Del.: Glazier, 1981) 19–23.

THE NATURE OF THE GOSPELS

Another difficulty in knowing Jesus' originally intended meaning of a parable has to do with the nature of the Gospels in which the parables are found. In the first place, the Gospels are written documents, whereas the parables were originally communicated orally. The shift from oral communication to written affects meaning. In addition, the literary context in which a Gospel parable is placed may give it a different sense than it had in its original spoken context.

Moreover, the Gospels do not record the exact words of Jesus. The Gospel parables are two stages removed from the stories told by the earthly Jesus. Jesus' parables were preached by his followers, and underwent modifications in the retelling. As they took written form, some thirty to fifty years after Jesus' death, the parables were reshaped by each evangelist to meet the needs of his particular community of faith. The intent of the Gospel writers was not to preserve as accurately as possible the exact words of Jesus, rather they, like modern preachers, reinterpreted Jesus' stories for their new contexts. As a result, we find various versions of the same parable in different Gospels. Similar parables are placed in different settings, directed to different audiences, with resultant different meanings.

Analysis of the history of the traditions also reveals that often in the retelling of Jesus' parables moralizing and allegorizing tendencies were introduced. Whereas his original stories began as paradoxical challenges, they were many times tamed into illustrations of moral actions. It is necessary to sift through the layers of the tradition so as to uncover as best we can, the originally upsetting contrasts Jesus' stories presented.

THE NATURE OF OUR SOURCES OF KNOWLEDGE ABOUT THE ANCIENT WORLD

A further difficulty in knowing what Jesus intended to say and how his first audiences understood the parables is that our sources of knowledge about the ancient world are partial and incomplete. New discoveries from archaeology and of previously unknown manuscripts continue to enlighten us about the world of Jesus. Similarly, new methods of biblical interpretation bring to light fresh possibilities of meaning. Knowledge of the historical, social, economic, political, religious, and cultural world of Palestine and the Hellenistic world of the first century allows us to draw probable conclusions about a parable's original meaning, but the business of interpretation never rests on certitude.

METHODS OF PARABLE INTERPRETATION
ALLEGORICAL INTERPRETATION

The earliest approach to parable interpretation, the allegorical method,[4] is found in the Gospels themselves. This approach treats parables as allegories, that is, a series of metaphors in which each detail of the story is given a symbolic meaning. The first biblical example concerns the parable of the sower and the seed (Mark 4:1-9 and pars.). The allegorical explanation in Mark 4:13-20 and pars. is that the seed is the word and the different types of soil represent the various ways that people hear and respond to the word. The seed that falls on the path represents those whose hearing is quickly derailed by Satan; those on rocky ground have no root and quickly fall away when tribulation comes; for those sown among thorns the word is choked off by worldly anxiety; those on rich soil hear and accept the word and bear abundant fruit. A similar allegorical interpretation of the parable of the weeds and the wheat (Matt 13:24-30) is found in Matthew 13:36-43.[5] Most scholars recognize these as interpretations of the early faith communities, and not from Jesus himself.

The allegorical approach was the preferred method of patristic and medieval biblical scholars. From Origen (second century C.E.) until the rise of modern biblical criticism, this method held sway. A good example is the interpretation of the parable of the Good Samaritan (Luke 10:29-37) used by Augustine and others: the traveler is Adam, representing human-

---

[4] See Carolyn Osiek, "Literal Meaning and Allegory," *TBT* 29/5 (1991) 261–66; Barbara Reid, "Once Upon a Time . . . Parable and Allegory in the Gospels," *TBT* 29/5 (1991) 267–72.

[5] Another pre-critical approach is proof-texting, which was used to interpret this parable in medieval times as justification for the burning of heretics.

kind. He descends from Jerusalem, the lost paradise, to Jericho, that is, the world. The robbers are evil spirits that deprive him of virtue and immortality. That he is left half dead means that he is alive insofar as he can know God, but dead in that he is in the power of sin. The priest and Levite are the law and the prophets of Israel, unable to help. The Samaritan is Christ, outsider to the theological claims of Israel. His animal is the body of Christ, on which are borne the sins of humanity. The inn is the Church, where oil and wine, the sacraments, heal the traveler's wounds. The inn-keeper, representing the apostles, is authorized to continue caring for the wounded man until the return of the Samaritan, that is, until the second coming of Christ.[6]

ONE MAIN POINT

At the end of the nineteenth century the German biblical scholar Adolph Jülicher[7] revolutionized the study of parables by arguing that a parable has only one main point. With the dawn of historical critical methods, Jülicher further insisted that the point must be sought in the historical context of the teaching of Jesus.

Since that time there has been much debate over whether there was any allegorical dimension at all to the original parables of Jesus. Some scholars contend that all allegorical elements are the later interpretations by the evangelists or the early Christian communities from whom they received the parables. Other exegetes do not so rigidly distinguish between parable and allegory. They argue that the Gospel parables are allegorical in nature if one understands allegory not as a series of metaphors, but as an extended metaphor in narrative form.

MORE OR LESS ALLEGORICAL

One difference from earlier allegorical interpretation is that critics today do not try to find symbolism behind as many details. In addition, they attempt to find meanings that would

---

[6] See, e.g., Irenaeus, *Adversus haereses* III.17,3.
[7] Adolph Jülicher, *Die Gleichnisreden Jesu* (2 vols.; Tübingen: Mohr [Siebeck] 1888, 1899).

be intelligible in Jesus' day. One solution is to think of parables on a sliding scale of more or less allegorical.[8] There is a further difficulty with Jülicher's insistence that there is *one* main point in a parable. With many interpretations possible, how can we know which is *the* main point originally intended? It may be that each main character (human or not) in a parable may reveal an important point.[9] For example, in the sower parable (Mark 4:1-9 and pars.) if the sower is the focus, the point is God's lavish generosity (through Jesus' preaching, teaching, and healing) in sowing the Word on all kinds of soil, good and bad alike. If the focus is the seed, the message is that the Word is effective. Despite early failure or unremarkable initial results, it will eventually bear fruit in abundance. If the soil is the focal point, as in the interpretation in Mark 4:13-20, then the emphasis is for believers to make sure to be fertile soil, cultivating themselves to be receptive and nurturing to the Word. Finally, if the harvest is highlighted, then the point is that the reign of God far exceeds all expectation. The explosiveness and grand scale of the yield, "thirty, sixty, and a hundredfold," is beyond anything a typical farmer experienced.

The task of the preacher is to discern *which* of the many possible points is the main one that the assembly needs to hear at this place and time. A significant contribution by Jülicher for preachers is the insight that a parable communicates best when it is told with one main point, or punchline, not as a series of metaphors.

PARABLES OF THE KINGDOM

Another significant contribution to modern parable interpretation was made by C. H. Dodd,[10] who argued that the par-

---

[8] Craig Blomberg, "Interpreting the Parables: Where Are We and Where Do We Go from Here?" *CBQ* 53 (1991) 50–78; *Interpreting the Parables* (Downers Grove, IL: InterVarsity Press, 1990) 29–69; and Kline Snodgrass, *The Parable of the Wicked Tenants* (Tübingen: Mohr [Siebeck] 1983) 13–26.

[9] Blomberg, *Interpreting*, 21, advances that most parables make three main points.

[10] Charles H. Dodd, *The Parables of the Kingdom* (London: Collins, 1961; first published by James Nisbet and Co., 1935).

ables be understood against the context of Jesus' eschatological proclamation. For him, all the parables convey the message that the kingdom of God is inaugurated and realized in Jesus. Scholars today question that a single lens, such as realized eschatology, is adequate to unfold all the rich dimensions of the parables.

HISTORICAL CRITICISM: GETTING TO THE ORIGINAL STORY

A very significant advance in parable interpretation came with the rise of historical critical methodology.[11] With the use of form and redaction criticism, in particular, historical critics investigate the kinds of alterations made in the transmission of the parables and attempt to recover the most primitive form. One of the most influential scholars in this century that employed this method in parables research was Joachim Jeremias.[12] He identified ten principles of transformation by which the early church adapted Jesus' parables to their own situation: (1) translation from Aramaic to Greek, (2) shift from a Palestinian to a Hellenistic environment, (3) embellishment of details, (4) remodeling along the lines of Old Testament and folk-story themes, (5) change of audience from interested crowds or opponents to disciples, (6) shift from a warning to the multitude about the gravity of the eschatological crisis to a hortatory use to direct the conduct of Christians, (7) metaphors assume greater Christological and ecclesial significance, (8) allegorization of details, (9) tendency toward collection and conflation, and (10) placement in a secondary setting. Recognizing these tendencies in the transmission of the tradition, and using his vast knowledge of first-century Palestine, Jeremias worked to uncover the original words and settings of the parables of Jesus.

---

[11] See Edgar Krentz, *The Historical-Critical Method* (Guides to Biblical Scholarship; Philadelphia: Fortress, 1975).
   [12] Joachim Jeremias, *The Parables of Jesus*, 8th ed. (New York: Scribner's, 1972). Similarly, Rudolph Bultmann, *History of the Synoptic Tradition*, rev. ed. (New York: Harper & Row, 1968); A. T. Cadoux, *The Parables of Jesus* (London: James Clarke, 1931).

This method is still extremely valuable to try to determine what was the original form of Jesus' parables and in what historical context they were spoken. This is one important step in a preacher's preparation. But the task of the preacher goes beyond simply recounting what the story meant in Jesus' day.

SOCIAL-SCIENCE APPROACH

Closely related to historical critical methods is the recently developed science of social study of the New Testament.[13] This area of study engages biblical scholars, experts in social science, classicists, and ancient historians, who collaborate to reconstruct not only the history, but also the economic, social, and political life of Greek and Roman civilizations of the first centuries before and after Christ. They use art, contemporary literature, inscriptions, coins, and archaeological finds to gain knowledge of the institutions, social dynamics, and horizons of consciousness of people who lived at the time of Jesus.

An example is Richard Rohrbaugh's reading of the parable of the talents/pounds (Matt 25:14-20; Luke 19:11-27).[14] Reading from the point of view of a peasant of a first century Mediterranean agrarian society rather than with the assumptions of a capitalist from the West, the parable results as a warning to those who mistreat the poor, not to those who lack adventurous industry.

One caution about this method is that it is a modern construction, not devised specifically for biblical study. A question remains: how well can it be applied to ancient texts and societies? Nonetheless, this approach opens up fresh meanings and can offer satisfactory solutions for details that other methods leave as inexplicable. It can also advance new possibilities for

---

[13] See Carolyn Osiek, *What Are They Saying About the Social Setting of the New Testament?* (2d ed. New York: Paulist, 1992); Bruce J. Malina and Richard L. Rohrbaugh, *Social-Science Commentary on the Synoptic Gospels* (Minneapolis: Fortress, 1992); John J. Pilch, *The Cultural World of Jesus. Sunday by Sunday, Cycle B* (Collegeville: The Liturgical Press, 1996).

[14] Richard L. Rohrbaugh, "A Peasant Reading of the Parable of the Talents/Pounds: A Text of Terror?" *BTB* 23 (1993) 32–39.

action in the contemporary world that would lead to genuine social change.

LITERARY APPROACHES

Another turning point in parable study came in the 1960s with the work of Amos Wilder and Robert Funk, who moved into methods of literary interpretation.[15] They explore the aesthetics of the language in the parables, their poetry, imagery, and symbolism. They analyze how metaphor moves from a literary figure to a theological and hermeneutical category, providing a key to a new understanding of the parables.

A related direction of literary study is narrative criticism.[16] This approach analyzes the plot, character development, point of view, and dramatic movement of the story apart from its historical context. Narrative criticism also attends to the response evoked by the text in the reader.

Rhetorical criticism has also become an important tool for analyzing parables as persuasive speech. This method studies how the type of argument, its arrangement, and its style of presentation bring about the desired effect.

Finally, semiotic or structuralist methods[17] have been applied to the parables, although most people find them too complicated and diffuse to be of help. The aim is to uncover the deep structures of meaning through analysis of the synchronic structure. Grids delineating the subject, object, sender, recipient, helper, and opponent are employed to this end.

---

[15] Robert Funk, *Language, Hermeneutic, and Word of God* (New York: Harper & Row, 1966); *Parables and Presence* (Philadelphia: Fortress, 1982); Amos Wilder, *The Language of the Gospel* (New York: Harper & Row, 1964); *Jesus' Parables and the War of Myths* (Philadelphia: Fortress, 1982). John Dominic Crossan (*In Parables: The Challenge of the Historical Jesus* [New York: Harper & Row, 1973]; *The Dark Interval* [Sonoma: Polebridge, 1988]) bridges two methods when he begins with tradition-critical considerations and then moves to a literary metaphorical approach.

[16] E.g., Dan O. Via, *The Parables: Their Literary and Existential Dimension* (Philadelphia: Fortress, 1967). See also Mark A. Powell, *What is Narrative Criticism?* (Guides to Biblical Scholarship; Philadelphia: Fortress, 1990).

[17] See Daniel Patte, *What Is Structural Exegesis?* (Guides to Biblical Scholarship; Philadelphia: Fortress, 1976).

Literary methods deal with the finished form of the text as we have it, not the process through which it has come. They recognize that meaning is constructed in the interaction between text and reader, quite apart from the original intention of the author. They can be very useful in showing the ongoing function of the parable in any context to invite participation in Jesus' understanding of God and the divine realm.

LIBERATION APPROACHES

This approach to biblical interpretation was born in Latin America some three decades ago.[18] Its underlying principle is that reflection on experience precedes theoretical analysis. And it is the experience of people who are poor and oppressed that is the starting point. The second step is critical analysis of the social and political causes of oppression. In the process a correlation is sought between the present situation and biblical stories of deliverance and liberation. The final move is to strategize and act for liberation. This method relies on the faithful reflection of ordinary people of faith, not solely or even primarily on that of biblical scholars. It is a communal endeavor that seeks to embody God's word of justice and hope in this world, here and now.

With regard to parable interpretation, this method challenges approaches that would claim to discover universal messages in Jesus' stories, applied and reapplied from one generation to the next and from one social context to another. It asks questions like: "What if the parables of Jesus were neither theological nor moral stories but political and economic ones? What if the concern of the parables was not the reign of God but the reigning systems of oppression that dominated Palestine in the time of Jesus? What if the parables are exposing exploitation rather than revealing justification?"[19]

[18] See Christopher Rowland and Mark Corner, *Liberating Exegesis. The Challenge of Liberation Theology to Biblical Studies* (Louisville: Westminster/John Knox, 1989); Clodovis Boff and Jorge Pixley, *The Bible, the Church, and the Poor* (Theology and Liberation Series; Maryknoll, N.Y.: Orbis, 1989); Carlos Mesters, *Defenseless Flower. A New Reading of the Bible* (Maryknoll, N.Y.: Orbis, 1989).

[19] Willaim R. Herzog II, *Parables as Subversive Speech. Jesus as Pedagogue of the Oppressed* (Louisville: Westminster/John Knox, 1994) 7.

A drawback to this approach is that some find that the kind of study required of social and political structures as well as of biblical and ecclesial tradition is too much to ask of simple believers. For some there is more solace in an approach that provides sure doctrines, simple morality, literal, authoritative interpretations of the Bible, and an assurance of future reward for enduring present oppression and suffering.

An advantage to this method is that it can be used in tandem with historical, social science, and literary methods, while providing the lens through which to view the text. It is an invaluable tool for engaging Jesus' stories in a new context in a way that can challenge the unjust structures in our day and bring good news to those oppressed. The danger, of course, is that one who would preach this way risks rejection and persecution as did the first proclaimer of the parables.

CONCLUSION

No one method provides the definitive key. Each contributes significantly to our understanding of what the parables meant, how they convey their meaning, and what they can mean for us today. It is important for a preacher to know what method a biblical commentator is using, so as to understand what results it will yield. Likewise, preachers themselves should consciously choose the hermeneutical model by which they construct their preaching.[20]

The next chapter gives an overview of the Gospel of Mark. Subsequent chapters deal with the parables in the order in which they appear in the lectionary. Attention will be given to how various methods result in different meanings. The focus is biblical interpretation, only one of the many tasks of the preacher. It remains for the preacher to discern which approach conveys the needed message for the particular assembly gathered in a specific place and time.

[20] See Raymond Bailey, ed. *Hermeneutics for Preaching. Approaches to Contemporary Interpretations of Scripture* (Nashville: Broadman, 1992); Mary Margaret Pazdan, "Hermeneutics and Proclaiming the Sunday Readings," *In The Company of Preachers* (Collegeville: The Liturgical Press, 1993) 26–37.

CHAPTER THREE

Overview of the Gospel of Mark

RETRIEVING THE CONTEXT

In his book *The Gates of the Forest* Elie Wiesel tells this story: "When the great Rabbi Israel Baal Shem-Tov saw misfortune threatening the Jews it was his custom to go into a certain part of the forest to meditate. There he would light a fire, say a special prayer, and the miracle would be accomplished and the misfortune averted."

"Later, when his disciple, the celebrated Magid of Mezritch, had occasion, for the same reason, to intercede with heaven, he would go to the same place in the forest and say: 'Master of the Universe, listen! I do not know how to light the fire, but I am still able to say the prayer.' And again the miracle would be accomplished."

"Still later, Rabbi Moshe-Leib of Sasov, in order to save his people once more, would go into the forest and say: 'I do not know how to light the fire, I do not know the prayer, but I know the place and this must be sufficient.' It was sufficient and the miracle was accomplished."

"Then it fell to Rabbi Israel of Rizhyn to overcome misfortune. Sitting in his armchair, his head in his hands, he spoke to God: 'I am unable to light the fire and I do not know the prayer; I cannot even find the place in the forest. All I can do is to tell the story, and this must be sufficient.' And it was sufficient."[1]

Wiesel's account illustrates the power of stories, even when the details of their original context are lost. This is the situation we face when trying to retrieve the original settings and meanings of Jesus' parables. The form in which they have come to

[1] Elie Wiesel, *The Gates of the Forest* (tr., Frances Frenaye; New York: Holt, Rinehart and Winston, 1966) i–iii.

25

us is now three stages removed from their first telling. Like Rabbi Israel of Rizhyn, all we have is the story. To understand the meaning of a parable, it would be most helpful if we could retrieve the contexts in which it was shaped and reshaped. To that end, we will sketch briefly the setting and situation of Mark's community as best can be determined from our current "armchairs."

NEWFOUND POPULARITY

For many centuries the Gospel of Mark suffered neglect. Augustine thought it merely a summary of Matthew,[2] and regarded the latter far more useful for catechesis. The style of Mark's Gospel was thought to be crude in comparison to the lofty poetic style of the Fourth Gospel, or the refined Greek of the Gospel of Luke. Only in the last two or three decades has there been a renewed interest in Mark. This interest has taken a variety of forms. Literary and narrative studies of the Gospel have opened up new understandings of Mark as a masterfully crafted story. The characters are unforgettable and the movement of the plot, with its careful foreshadowings and recapitulations draws one relentlessly to its powerful climax. Scholars now recognize that the author has imbedded in the narrative memorization aids for oral recitation, which is how the Gospel first would have been communicated.[3]

There has also been a spate of socio-political studies of Mark's Gospel. Scholars now recognize that the relentless shadow of the cross and the rawness of the crucified Jesus in this Gospel communicate a sober indictment of oppressive political regimes and a powerful message of hope to those most downtrodden when read from a perspective of liberation hermeneutics.

---

[2] Augustine, *On the Agreement of the Evangelists*, 1.2.4.

[3] Among those who have committed the entire Gospel to memory are actor Alec McCowen (*Personal Mark. An Actor's Proclamation of St. Mark's Gospel* [New York: Crossroads, 1985]) and Professor David Rhoads of the Lutheran School of Theology at Chicago. Videotapes of his oral presentation are available from "SELECT," 2199 East Main Street, Columbus, Ohio 43209.

AUTHOR

Who was the author of this Gospel? As was usual in antiquity, he did not sign or date his manuscript, nor identify the locale. Much of what we can surmise is from clues in the text, but there are few sure answers.[4]

John Mark

Tradition has identified the evangelist with John Mark, whose mother Mary had a house in Jerusalem, where Christians assembled (Acts 12:12). A cousin of Barnabas (Col 4:10), John Mark accompanied Barnabas and Paul on their missionary journey to Cyprus and as far as Antioch in Pisidia (Acts 12:25–13:13). In Paul's Letter to Philemon (v. 24) he conveys greetings from Mark, a coworker. And in 2 Timothy 4:11 Paul tells Timothy to bring Mark to Rome. There is also mention of Mark, who sends greetings along with Peter in 1 Peter 5:13. The question is whether the Mark mentioned in these other references is the person who penned the Gospel. Most modern scholars reject the identification of John Mark with the evangelist.[5]

Peter's Interpreter

There are numerous references in the writings of the early Church Fathers that Mark received the tradition from Peter. Eusebius quotes from a lost work (ca. 135 C.E.) of Papias, bishop of Hierapolis in Asia Minor, who says that an elder named John conveyed to him that, "Mark, having become the interpreter of Peter, wrote down accurately everything that he remembered, without however recording in order what was either said or done by Christ. For neither did he hear the Lord, nor did he follow Him; but afterwards, as I said, [attended] Peter, who adapted his instructions to the needs [of his hearers] but had no design of giving a connected account of the Lord's oracles. So then

[4] For an excellent summary of the various views on Mark over the centuries see "The Lives of Mark" by Janice Capel Anderson and Stephen D. Moore in *Mark and Method. New Approaches in Biblical Studies* (ed. J. C. Anderson and S. Moore; Minneapolis: Fortress, 1992) 1–22.

[5] An exception is Martin Hengel, *Studies in the Gospel of Mark* (Philadelphia: Fortress, 1985).

Mark made no mistake, while he thus wrote down some things as he remembered them; for he made it his own care not to omit anything that he had heard, or to set down any false statement therein" (*Historia Ecclesiastica* 3.39.15).

Of course we must ask, was Papias in a position to know positively about the identity of the evangelist? Did other Church Fathers have independent evidence? Or did they all originate from Papias' testimony? One curiosity is that if Peter is the source for Mark's Gospel, why is he not portrayed in a more prominent or positive light in it? Compare, for example, Jesus' response to Peter's proclamation of faith in Matthew 16:17-19 to Mark 8:30. In the latter there is no saying of Jesus building his kingdom on Peter the "rock" nor is he given the keys to the kingdom of heaven, as in Matthew. It is possible that the connection with Peter was made so as to lend the Gospel the apostolic authority it needed in the formative years of early Christianity.

An Anonymous Second-Generation Christian

What we can surmise about the author from the Gospel itself is that he was a Greek-speaking, second-generation Christian. The Gospel was written in Greek, but the author clearly understands Aramaic and/or Hebrew. He translates Aramaic or Hebrew phrases such as *Boanērges* into Greek, *huioi brontēs*, that is, "sons of thunder" (3:17-19), or *talitha koum, to korasion, soi legō, egeire*, meaning, "little girl, I say to you, arise!" (5:41).[6]

He is a second-generation Christian, not an eyewitness, as is clear from the kinds of concerns addressed in the Gospel. For the sake of convention, we will continue to call the evangelist "Mark," although his identity remains unknown.

WHEN

The big debate is whether Mark was writing before or after the fall of the Temple in 70 C.E. The decision partly rests on how one interprets chapter 13. Does it foretell what is about to happen? Or does it describe what has already occurred? Those

---

[6] See also 7:11; 10:46; 11:9-10; 14:32, 36, 45; 15:22, 34.

who argue for a pre-70 date point out that the imagery and language could have been taken from the book of Daniel and other apocalyptic literature; it need not presuppose the actual destruction of the Temple. Moreover, Mark 9:1 and 13:30 express the expectation of an imminent parousia, which points toward an early date. Other scholars hold that it was written in the immediate aftermath of the Jewish War to Jewish Christians to give them courage at a time when they might come under suspicion as potential revolutionaries.

WHERE

There are a number of suggestions for the locale of the community for whom Mark wrote. The oldest tradition puts them in Rome. Many contemporary scholars still find this the most persuasive hypothesis. There are a number of transliterated Latin words in the Gospel, e.g., *legiōn* (5:9), *dēnariōn* (6:37), and *kodrantēs* (12:42). The latter refers to the *quadrans*, a coin used in Rome, not in Syria nor in Galilee. Many think that Mark is not familiar with Palestinian geography as 7:31 implies that Tyre is north of Sidon. And Mark 10:11-12 presumes a non-Jewish context where women have the right to initiate divorce. That Mark's audience is predominantly Gentile is evident from the way that the evangelist has to explain Jewish customs to them (e.g., 7:3-4, 11). One of the most persuasive reasons to locate Mark in Rome is the theological critique of abusive power that his Gospel offers. A setting at the heart of imperial power is logical.

Scholars such as Willi Marxsen[7] and Werner Kelber[8] have suggested Galilee as the locale. In the Gospel, Galilee is the place of initial revelation and of the first successful reception of Jesus' healing and preaching. The final instruction of the heavenly messenger to the disciples is that Jesus is going before them to Galilee and there they will see him (16:7). Such an emphasis is explainable if the evangelist's community is located there.

---

[7] Willi Marxsen, *Mark the Evangelist: Studies on the Redaction History of the Gospel* (Nashville: Abingdon, 1969).
[8] Werner Kelber, *The Kingdom in Mark: A New Place and a New Time* (Philadelphia: Fortress, 1974).

One other suggestion offered by Howard Clark Kee[9] is southern Syria. Such a locale would fit the profile of an apocalyptic community manifest in the atmosphere of the Gospel. What Kee interprets as Mark's antipathy toward cities and less cultured style of Greek would fit rural Syria. Recently Richard Rohrbaugh, from his analysis of the social stratification apparent in Mark's Gospel, has argued that the Marcan audience was composed largely of non-literate peasants in a village or small town context either in the rural areas of southern Syria, Transjordan, or Upper Galilee.[10]

In her rhetorical study of the Gospel, Mary Ann Beavis finds that Mark closely resembles a five-act Hellenistic play in terms of plot and structure. This has implications for the social setting of the Gospel. She proposes that the evangelist was a Christian missionary and teacher who composed the Gospel for use in missionary preaching. His Greco-Roman audience was composed of both Christians and potential converts. Since the characters of whom Jesus approves in the Gospel are common people, particularly the poor, sick, Gentiles, and women, it is probable that these made up the bulk of the audience.[11]

SOURCES

Most scholars hold that Mark is the first of the Gospels to be written and that Matthew and Luke have relied on Mark as one of their sources.[12] Mark was both a creative author and faithful to the traditions he received. It is most probable that he received bodies of tradition already in written form. Most likely the passion narrative came to him already as a continuous narrative. Clusters of miracle stories, parables, and controversy

---

[9] Howard Clark Kee, *Community of the New Age: Studies in Mark's Gospel* (Philadelphia: Westminster, 1977).

[10] Richard L. Rohrbaugh, "The Social Location of the Markan Audience," *Int* 47 (1993) 380–95.

[11] Mary Ann Beavis, *Mark's Audience. The Literary and Social Setting of Mark 4.11-12* (JSNTSup 33; Sheffield: JSOT Press, 1989).

[12] There is, however a contemporary renewal led by William R. Farmer (*The Synoptic Problem: A Critical Analysis* [New York: Macmillan, 1964]) of the hypothesis first proposed in the eighteenth century by Johann Griesbach that Luke relied on Matthew as a source and that Mark is an abridgement of the two.

stories were already formulated in units before Mark set about his writing. He was not, however, simply a scissors-and-paste man, but exercised creative authorial freedom in reshaping and retelling the tradition so as to meet the pressing needs of his own community.

The traditions that came to Mark had also been shaped by the oral preaching and by liturgical use. Benoit Standaert[13] envisions the post-70 Easter Vigil celebrated in Rome as the setting that shaped Mark. This would account for the strong baptismal and paschal imagery in the Gospel (e.g., 1:1-13; 10:38; 16:5).

GENRE

Mark opens his narrative, "The beginning of the gospel (*euangelion*, "good news"*) of Jesus Christ [the Son of God]" (1:1). By contrast, Matthew begins "the book (*biblos*) of the genealogy of Jesus Christ." Luke sets out to give a "narrative" (*diēgēsis*). John's introduction stresses "testimony" or "witness" (*martyria*, 1:7, 15). Each evangelist has a slightly different manner of presenting the Gospel story, as is clear from their various introductions. The question of the literary genre of the Gospel, particularly that of Mark, is one that has drawn the attention of scholars in recent times.

Mark did not invent the term "gospel" (*euangelion*). In Greek literature the word was used to denote the report brought by a herald.[14] In the Greco-Roman world *euangelion* referred to announcements of victory or great events in the life of the emperor. In the Septuagint the term is used in a profane sense, as when David refers to news of Saul's death as "good news" (2 Sam 4:10). It is used also in reference to the good news of God's sovereign rule, as in Isaiah 52:7, "How beautiful upon the mountains are the feet of the messenger who announces peace, who brings good news, who announces salvation, who says to Zion, 'Your God reigns'" (NRSV).

While the term itself was common parlance, was the gospel genre something new? In earlier studies, the gospel was thought to be a unique literary form invented by Mark.

---

[13] Benoit Standaert, *L'Évangile selon Marc* (Lire la Bible 61; Paris: Cerf, 1983).

[14] E.g., Homer's *Odyssey* 14.152,166.

More recently scholars have compared Mark with other contemporary literature. Some see Mark as a type of Greco-Roman
biography, such as Andronicus' *Life of Aristotle* (ca. 70 B.C.E.) or
Philo's *Life of Moses* (ca. 25 B.C.E.).[15] The reader of such didactic
biographies was meant to learn from the exemplary figure
how to order one's life and emulate it. These biographies functioned to confirm the authority of the great figure or to defend
him against misunderstanding.

Other scholars propose that Mark be read as history, such
as Chronicles, or Josephus' *Antiquities of the Jews*. This genre
focuses on the significant acts of great persons in the political
and social spheres. Adela Yarbro Collins proposes that Mark's
purpose was to write a specific kind of history: one that nar-
rates the course of eschatological events.[16] Such an apocalyptic
history would seek to show "God's creation with a 'develop-
mental history' and a destiny."[17]

There are those who see the whole Gospel narrative as
parable.[18] The whole account, not only the individual parables,
functions to shock, reverse expectations, shatter the world of
the hearer, and call for conversion. The objection can be raised,
however, that such a function does not qualify as a separate
genre; proverbs, miracle stories, ethical teachings, and the like,
can all have this function as well.[19]

---

[15] E.g., David Aune, "Greco-Roman Biography" in *Greco-Roman Literature
and the New Testament* (ed. D. Aune; Atlanta: Scholars Press, 1988) 107–26;
Charles Talbert, "Once Again: Gospel Genre," in *Genre, Narrativity and Theology* (Ed. Mary Gerhart and James G. Williams; Semeia 43; Atlanta: Scholars
Press, 1988) 53–73.

[16] Adela Yarbro Collins, "Is Mark's Gospel a Life of Jesus? The Question
of Genre," in *The Beginning of the Gospel. Probings of Mark in Context* (Minneapolis: Fortress, 1992) 1–38.

[17] Ibid., 38.

[18] E.g., John Dominic Crossan, *The Dark Interval* (Niles, IL: Argus, 1975)
126; John R. Donahue, "Jesus as the Parable of God in the Gospel of Mark," *Int*
32 (1978) 369–86; Werner Kelber, *The Oral and Written Gospel* (Philadelphia:
Fortress, 1983); James G. Williams, *Gospel Against Parable: Mark's Language of
Mystery* (Sheffield: Almond, 1985). See Elizabeth Struthers Malbon, "Mark:
Myth and Parable," *BTB* 16 (1986) 8–17, where she proposes that both im-
pulses are integrated in Mark. The Gospel both comforts by confirming the established world (myth) and subverts (parable).

[19] Talbert, "Gospel Genre," 73.

STRUCTURE

Three-Stage Linear Movement

In recent years there has been a shift in how scholars perceive the structure of Mark's Gospel. Earlier analyses saw the story moving in a linear progression in three movements. The first movement in chapters 1–8 is driven by the mystery of Jesus' identity. Only the demons and unclean spirits know who Jesus is (1:24; 3:11; 5:7). The human characters in the drama puzzle over who he is when he heals and forgives sins (2:7), when he exercises power over nature (4:41; 6:49-50), and when he teaches with authority (1:27; 6:3). Herod mistakenly decides that Jesus is John brought back to life (6:14-16). The first climax comes when Jesus puts the question to his disciples, "Who do you say that I am?" (8:29). At this juncture Peter's response, "You are the Messiah" (8:30) is affirmed, but immediately shown to be inadequate.

Jesus' first prediction of his passion and his rebuke of Peter (8:31-33) launches the second movement of the story, where the overarching question is "What kind of Messiah?" The three passion predictions and the teachings on discipleship spell out that Jesus is a Messiah that suffers and dies. The second climax comes at the confession of the centurion at the cross, "Truly this man was the Son of God!" (Mark 15:39).

Stage three begins with the proclamation of the resurrection (16:6-7) and continues in the life of believers who announce the good news and carry it forth in their lives.

In this delineation of Mark, the structure is both theological and geographical. The first movement takes place in Galilee, where Jesus' identity is shrouded in mystery. In this first section Jesus' ministry is directed to a wide group of people, some of whom follow him and some of whom reject him. In the second part Jesus' identity and mission are more explicitly spelled out. The audience narrows, as Jesus addresses primarily those who are already followers. The journey is relentlessly toward Jerusalem. The final stage directs the disciples back to Galilee (16:7), the place of revelation and of parousia. This structure can be shown as follows:

16:1-8 Third Movement: The Risen Messiah
    /   The revelation continues in the life of believers
15:39 Second Climax: Suffering, Dying Messiah
    /   What Kind of Messiah?
8:27-30 First Climax: "You are the Messiah"
    /   Who is this?
1:1 Jesus' identity revealed to the reader

Concentric, Chiastic Framework

More recently scholars have discerned patterns of chiasm and ring composition in Mark. Patterns of repetition, foreshadowing, recapitulation, framing, and inclusio, both aid in the oral proclamation of the narrative and in the understanding of the separate units in relation to the whole. One such analysis is that of Augustine Stock, who sees a five-fold geographical framework that is concentric.[20] It can be illustrated as follows.

I. Prologue   II. Galilee   III. The Way   IV. Jerusalem   V. Epilogue

1:1-13   1:14–8:26   8:27–10:52   11:1–15:41   15:42–16:8

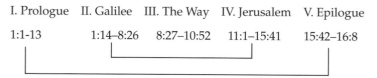

In this schema the five sections are linked by either continuity or contrast and are held together by five hinge pieces (1:14-15; 8:22-26; 10:46-52; 15:40-41) that point both backward and forward. The first and last sections are yoked by continuity: both take place in the wilderness and feature a messenger (John the Baptist in the prologue and the young man clad in

---

[20] Augustine Stock, *The Method and Message of Mark* (Wilmington, Del.: Glazier, 1989). This structure was first identified by Benoit Standaert, *L'Evangile selon Marc: Composition et genre littéraire* (Brugge: Sint Andriesabdij, 1978) and further developed by Bas van Iersel, *Reading Mark*, tr. W. H. Bisscheroux (Collegeville: The Liturgical Press, 1988). See also Franz Neirynck, *Duality in Mark. Contributions to the Study of the Markan Redaction* (BETL 31; Leuven: Leuven University Press, 1972) and Joanna Dewey, *Markan Public Debate: Literary Technique, Concentric Structure, and Theology in Mark 2:1-3:6* (SBLDS 48; Chico, Calif.: Scholars Press, 1980).

white in the epilogue) who announces good news. From these places of death come the beginnings of new life. The second and fourth parts are set in contrast. In part two Galilee is the place of revelation and successful gathering of disciples. This is an unexpected twist; one would expect Jerusalem to play this role. Rather, in part four Jerusalem is the place that rejects the Christ and puts him to death. The center of the narrative is the journey on the way between Galilee and Jerusalem. It features three predictions of the passion and is framed by two stories of healing of men who were blind (8:22-26; 10:46-52). These bookends give hope that, despite the great difficulty entailed in "seeing" Jesus and following him, disciples can, indeed, perceive well enough to live the mystery in his footsteps.

THE ENDING

The ending of Mark's Gospel is quite an enigma. Most ancient manuscripts end with 16:8 where the women, having found the tomb empty and having been commissioned by the messenger in white to go and tell the disciples that Jesus is going before them to Galilee, flee from the tomb and say nothing to anyone because they are afraid. Has the ending been lost? Was Mark prevented from finishing the story? Why are there no resurrection appearances as in the other Gospels? Many different solutions have been proposed over the centuries.

That ancient copyists did not think that 16:8 was the true ending of the Gospel is evident from the various endings found in different manuscripts. Several of these are included in the canonical Gospel. The "Longer Ending" (Mark 16:9-20) is not found in the best and earliest manuscripts now available. The content is borrowed from the resurrection appearances found in Luke 24 and John 20. Its vocabulary and style clearly show that it was written by someone other than the evangelist, probably in the second century.

The "Shorter Ending," which also employs non-Marcan language, is found after 16:8 and before vv. 19-20 in four manuscripts that date to the seventh through ninth centuries. It is also found in one Old Latin version without the "longer ending." One other manuscript that dates to the fourth or fifth century and is housed in the Freer Gallery in Washington, D.C., adds a gloss after v. 14 that softens the rebuke of the disciples for their unbelief.

These added endings provide a neater closure to the story and bring Mark's ending into closer conformity with the conclusions of the other three canonical gospels. However, narrative critics recognize that such re-writes ruin the impact of the very powerful original ending at 16:8. Whereas the evangelist left the story open-ended, demanding that the hearers bring it to completion in their lives, the secondary endings render the hearer passive, giving neat resolution to all the ambiguity and human struggle embodied in the fearful disciples. It is preferable to see the whole Gospel as an open-ended parable whose meaning must be wrestled with and whose interpretative possibilities are never completely closed off.

THEOLOGICAL EMPHASES

One of the salient features of the Gospel of Mark is the emphasis on suffering. The shadow of the cross looms large in almost every passage. Controversies over Jesus' healings and breaking of the sabbath already escalate to a death plot in 3:6. The passion of Jesus is told in the starkest possible tones. There is no comforting angel in Gethsemane as in Luke 22:43-44. On the cross there is no peaceful handing over of Jesus' life, as in Luke 22:46 or John 19:30. The Marcan Jesus seems to die without comfort, totally abandoned, as he calls out, "My God, my God, why have you forsaken me?" (15:34). Most likely this Gospel was addressed originally to a community that was facing persecution themselves. Seeing their own story in that of Jesus would be a source of hope and encouragement. The One who had preceded them in suffering and death had conquered even death itself and now goes ahead of them to bring new life.

Related to this emphasis on the cross is also the question of power. Jesus is portrayed as the "strong man" (Mark 3:27-28) whose power is manifest in the cross—which seems, paradoxically, the ultimate weakness. Abusive power is repeatedly denounced in this Gospel while divine power is revealed in restoration to wholeness. Jesus' followers are not to exercise domination over any other. The hallmark of greatness among disciples is exemplary service to one another (10:42-45), particularly to those seemingly of no account (9:36-37). The portrait of Jesus in Mark is a very human one. He is a man of strong emotions, ranging from compassion (1:44) to anger (3:5) to distressed sadness (14:33-34). He moves at a determined pace from healing to healing while proclaiming the realm of God. An aura of mystery surrounds him, as he repeatedly admonishes people not to tell of their healings or to reveal his identity. This secrecy motif keeps the hearer in suspense until the climactic revelation at the crucifixion. Only with the passion and empty tomb does Jesus' identity as suffering Messiah become clear. Only then can he be proclaimed.

The disciples are painted ambiguously. While they do continue to follow, they are often fearful (10:32) and frequently misunderstand Jesus and his mission.[21] They reject the notion of a Messiah that suffers (8:31-33) and seek places of honor for themselves (10:35-45). They betray Jesus (14:10-11) and abandon (14:50) and deny him (14:66-72). When Jesus commands silence, it is broken (1:44-45; 7:36) and when the faithful women are told to proclaim they do not fulfill the command (16:8). In this Gospel no disciple is perfect; all struggle to understand, all struggle to follow. For contemporary disciples who wrestle with trying to understand God's ways and with trying to follow Jesus, this Gospel offers hope.

MARCAN PARABLES IN THE LECTIONARY

The Gospel of Mark has far fewer parables than the Gospels of Matthew and Luke. Almost all the Marcan parables are clustered together in chapter four. There we find the parable of the sower (4:1-9) and its explanation (4:13-20); the sayings about the lamp, things hidden, and measurements (4:21-25); the seed growing of itself (4:26-29); and the parable of the mustard seed (4:30-32). Only these latter two appear in the Sunday lectionary (the eleventh Sunday of Ordinary Time). The others are found on two weekdays in week three of ordinary time. The

---

[21] See Mark 4:13, 41; 6:51; 7:17-18; 8:21, 32; 9:10, 34; 10:35-38.

other major Marcan parable is that of the wicked tenants (Mark 12:1-12), which appears on Monday of week nine of ordinary time. On four other Sundays there are enigmatic sayings that can be treated as parables: the old coat and new wine (Mark 2:18-22); the binding of a strong man (3:20-35); defilement from within (7:1-8, 14-15, 21-23), and the lesson of the fig tree (13:24-32). In the next chapters each one will be discussed in the order in which they appear in the lectionary, first the Sunday selections, then the weekday.

CHAPTER FOUR

Fasting, Old Coat, and New Wine
(Mark 2:18-22)

Eighth Sunday of Ordinary Time

The disciples of John and of the Pharisees were accustomed to fast.
People came to him and objected,
   "Why do the disciples of John and the disciples of the Pharisees fast,
      but your disciples do not fast?"
Jesus answered them,
   "Can the wedding guests fast while the bridegroom is with them?
As long as they have the bridegroom with them they cannot fast.
But the days will come when the bridegroom is taken away from them,
   and then they will fast on that day.
No one sews a piece of unshrunken cloth on an old cloak.
If he does, its fullness pulls away,
   the new from the old, and the tear gets worse.
Likewise, no one pours new wine into old wineskins.
Otherwise, the wine will burst the skins,
   and both the wine and the skins are ruined.
Rather, new wine is poured into fresh wineskins."

MARCAN LITERARY CONTEXT

Mark does not clearly label these sayings as a "parable," although Luke (5:36) does. However, Jesus' reply to his challengers in the Marcan text is clearly parabolic. As is often the case, Jesus responds to a direct challenge by backing off the controversial issue and by asking a question in figurative language. In this way he engages his opponents in active reflection that can lead to their conversion.

In the Gospel of Mark these parabolic sayings are at the center of a chain of five controversy stories that begin in Mark 2:1 and extend to Mark 3:6. They come on the heels of the opening chapter of the Gospel, where Jesus' ministry begins with an ideal day of healing, exorcising demons, proclaiming the reign of God, and gathering his first disciples. In the second chapter, conflict escalates in each of five episodes: the healing and forgiving of a man who was paralyzed (2:1-12); the call of Levi (2:13-17); the question of fasting (2:18-22); plucking grain on the sabbath (2:23-28); and the healing of a man with a withered hand (3:1-6). There is an interlocking structure[1] in which the first and last episodes frame the whole section with their focus on healing controversies. The first passage (2:1-12), which asserts Jesus' authority over sin, leads into Jesus' eating with sinners and calling such as Levi to discipleship (2:13-17). This then leads to the question of not fasting (2:18-22). The fourth episode (2:23-28) focuses on Jesus' authority over the sabbath, which culminates in the fifth pericope (3:1-6), in which he heals on a sabbath. At the center stands 2:18-22, which addresses the question of Jesus' relation to other religious leaders and the incompatibility of the old with the new. Herein is the thread that underlies all these controversial practices.

There is an escalating hostility between Jesus and his opponents in these five episodes. In the first the scribes only "questioned in their hearts" how Jesus can forgive sins (2:6). In the second they question Jesus' disciples about his practices (2:16). In the third and fourth they interrogate Jesus directly (2:18, 24). In the final incident Jesus preempts their attack by initiating the questions to them (3:4). The whole section concludes with the Pharisees and Herodians taking counsel against Jesus to put him to death (3:6). A first allusion to Jesus' death occurs in the saying about the bridegroom being taken away (2:20). From these early controversies the cross continues to cast its shadow across the whole of the Gospel of Mark.

---

[1] For some the structure is chiastic, e.g., Wilfrid Harrington, *Mark* (NTM 4; Wilmington, Del.: Glazier, 1979) 24–25; Augustine Stock, *The Method and Message of Mark* (Collegeville: The Liturgical Press, 1989) 90–92. For others, e.g., Joanna Dewey, "The Literary Structure of the Controversy Stories in Mark 2,1–3,6," *JBL* 92 (1973) 394–401; *Markan Public Debate* (SBLDS 48; Chico, Calif.: Scholars Press, 1980) 109–10, it is circular in structure.

HISTORICAL CONTEXT

It is probable that the five episodes in 2:1–3:6 were already connected in a pre-Marcan source. They have at their base historical episodes in the life of Jesus, but they have been shaped to address practical problems about mixed table fellowship, fasting, and sabbath observance that faced the Marcan community some thirty or forty years after Jesus' death. In Mark 2:18-22 two different situations are juxtaposed. The initial question put to Jesus (v. 18) and his answer (v. 19) concern the present practice of his disciples, that is, they do not fast, whereas disciples of John and those of the Pharisees do. In terms of historicity, this episode coheres with what we know of Jesus' practice elsewhere. In Matthew 11:18-19 and Luke 7:33-34, parallel passages from the Q source, there is the same contrast: the ascetical practice of John the Baptist, who neither eats nor drinks, is set against that of Jesus, who is dubbed "a glutton and a drunkard."[2] Against the fasting practices of other religious leaders, Jesus' eating habits were remarkable and caused speculation about his authority.

There is a shift in v. 20, where the question moves from justifying the present practice of Jesus and his disciples, to explaining why the church later took up the practice of fasting. For the Marcan community the problem was not *whether* they should fast or not. Rather, the challenge for them was to define themselves in relation to others, e.g., Pharisaic Jews and followers of John the Baptist, and to explain why their own practice of fasting differed from that of Jesus. In the Gospel the answers to these later questions are placed on the lips of Jesus, showing us the process of reinterpretation of the tradition for a new context that poses new questions.

The parabolic sayings about the old cloth and new wineskins in vv. 21-22 were probably independent maxims linked to vv. 18-20 prior to Mark's redaction.[3] In the present shape of

---

[2] In Matthew 4:2 // Luke 4:2 Jesus fasts for forty days in the desert in preparation for his ministry. Mark does not mention this in his version of the episode. Matthew and Luke give the impression that this was a one-time fast for a specific purpose and that fasting was not a regular practice of Jesus (see Matt 11:18-19; Luke 7:33-34).

[3] In the *Gospel of Thomas* §47 these two sayings are joined to other proverbs about the inability of a person to serve two masters.

the text, vv. 21-22 bring the questions about fasting to a climax. They assert the incompatibility of the old with the new and justify practices that deviate from those previously accepted.

THE NARRATIVE: JESUS' OPPONENTS

One of the elements in v. 18 that draws the attention of commentators is the mention of "disciples of the Pharisees." Many scholars remark that the phrase is unique and they puzzle over its meaning since the Pharisees did not have disciples.[4] There is another similar reference, however, in Matthew 22:16 where the Pharisees send "their disciples" to Jesus to ask about paying taxes to Caesar. Similarly, in Matthew 12:27 // Luke 11:19 Jesus asks the Pharisees, "If I cast out demons by Beelzebul, by whom do your sons *(hoi huioi hymōn)* cast them out?"[5] Here "your sons," as in Matthew 8:12 *(hoi huioi tēs basileias,* "sons of the kingdom")* denotes members of a group, that is, the equivalent of "those who belong to the Pharisees." Such a meaning is reinforced by Mark 2:19, where the expression *hoi huioi tou nymphōnos,* "sons of the bridegroom," denotes either "groomsmen" or "wedding guests." Further, it is likely that the phrase was constructed by Mark for the sake of parallelism with "the disciples of John" and for contrast with "your [Jesus'] disciples." The controversy focuses not on the practice of Jesus himself, but on that of his disciples, who are set in contrast to the disciples of John and those of the Pharisees.

While John the Baptist is introduced in the very opening lines of Mark's Gospel, this is the first mention of his disciples as a group. In Mark 1:6 John's diet is said to be locusts and wild honey. His asceticism is described in the context of his call for repentance and is therefore understood as a sign of penitence. In the narrative logic of the Gospel, John's disciples presumably share their leader's motive for fasting. Since John's death is not recounted until Mark 6:17-29, the reader does not presume that mourning is the motive for the fasting of John's disciples.

There are traces throughout the New Testament of rivalry in the early church between disciples of Jesus and those of John

---

[4] Harrington, *Mark*, 33.
[5] The translations in this paragraph are the author's own.

the Baptist (e.g., Matt 11:18-19 // Luke 7:33-34; Luke 1–2; John 1:6-8, 15, 19-23; Acts 19:1-7). Nonetheless the focus of the conflict in Mark 2:18-22 falls more heavily on that between Jesus and the Pharisees. In the controversies before and after 2:18-22 it is the Pharisees who are cast as Jesus' opponents. Their first appearance is in 2:16 where they question Jesus' eating with tax collectors and sinners. In 2:24 they accuse Jesus of letting his disciples do what is unlawful on the sabbath. The fifth episode in the series concludes with the Pharisees and Herodians looking for a way to put Jesus to death (3:6). Throughout the Gospel of Mark the Pharisees are continually set up as a foil to Jesus. In 7:1-23 they question Jesus about why his disciples eat with unclean hands. In 8:11 they seek a sign to test Jesus. In 10:2 they pose to Jesus a question about divorce, again to test him. Finally in 12:13 Pharisees and Herodians are sent to ensnare Jesus in his speech. It is remarkable that this is the last mention of the Pharisees in Mark. They do not appear in the passion narrative. Rather, the chief priests, elders, and scribes become the prime antagonists (14:53; 15:1).[6]

THE CONFLICT OVER FASTING

In the narrative the initial question concerns the reason why Jesus' disciples do not fast. They clearly stand out from the disciples of John and the Pharisees, who do fast, as well as the later followers of Jesus (v. 20) who subsequently take up the practice. The Jewish practice of fasting is long-standing. However, the only day on which fasting is required of all is Yom Kippur, the Day of Atonement (Lev 16:29; 23:27). This tradition likely dates to pre-exilic times. Other examples of fasting in the Hebrew Scriptures are individuals who fast so as to

---

[6] See further Elizabeth Struthers Malbon, "The Jewish Leaders in the Gospel of Mark. A Literary Study of Marcan Characterization," *JBL* 108/2 (1989) 259–81; Dieter Lührmann, "Die Pharisäer und die Schriftgelehrten im Markusevangelium," *ZNW* 78 (1987) 169–85; Robert Mowery, "Pharisees and Scribes, Galilee and Jerusalem," *ZNW* 80 (1989) 266–68; Anthony Saldarini, *Pharisees, Scribes, and Sadducees in Palestinian Society* (Wilmington, Del.: Glazier, 1988) 146–53. See Terence J. Keegan, "The Parable of the Sower and Mark's Jewish Leaders, *CBQ* 56 (1994) 501–18 and the references therein for further analysis of Jesus' opponents in the Gospel of Mark.

make their prayer of supplication more efficacious (Ps 35:13), or those who do so as an expression of penance (2 Sam 12:13-25; 1 Kgs 21:27) or mourning (2 Sam 1:12; 3:36). In Daniel 10:3 and later apocalyptic literature fasting is practiced to make one open to divine revelation or visions.

Among Jesus' contemporaries the Essenes were noted for their fasting, as attested by Josephus (*J.W.* 2.8.5), so also the Therapeuts in Egypt, as described by Philo (*VitaCont.* 34). In Luke's story of the Pharisee and the toll collector (Luke 18:9-18) the Pharisee prides himself on his twice-weekly fasting (v. 12). It is not certain whether this practice dates to pre-70 C.E. Pharisaism. Our earliest reference to the Pharisaic practice comes from the *Didache* (8:1),[7] where Christian fast days are set forth as Wednesday and Friday, in contrast to the Jewish fast days of Monday and Thursday.[8] Against such a backdrop, Jesus' non-fasting requires explanation.

THE BRIDEGROOM

Jesus' reply equates his disciples with wedding guests and himself with the bridegroom. This image recalls the many times in the prophetic literature where Yahweh is presented as the groom or the husband of the people of the covenant (e.g., Hos 2:19; Isa 54:3-6; 62:5; Jer 2:2; Ezekiel 16). One implication, then, is that Jesus is on a par with God who is also cast as bridegroom in the Hebrew Scriptures.[9] The use of the image, however, is not the same. In the prophetic texts, Yahweh is portrayed as faithful husband to perfidious Israel. The prophets urge Israel to repentance and return to their God who never breaks covenant trust. In Mark 2:19-20 the bridegroom's presence evokes joy and calls for suspension of all penitence.

There is also a stress on timing—the time of Jesus' earthly ministry is unique. The inbreaking of the reign of God brought

---

[7] The final form of the *Didache* dates to the first half of the second century.

[8] John Muddiman, "Fast, Fasting," in *Anchor Bible Dictionary* (ed. David N. Freedman; New York: Doubleday, 1997) 2.773–76.

[9] Other New Testament texts in which Jesus is presented as bridegroom or alluded to as such include: Matthew 22:1-14; 25:1-13; John 2:9-10; 3:29; 2 Corinthians 11:2; Ephesians 5:22-32; Revelation 18:23; 19:7, 9; 21:2, 9; 22:17.

by Jesus is like a marriage feast. It demands a temporary stop to all grieving and penitence for the time being. There is already a foretaste of Isaiah's prophecy about the messianic age, "On this mountain the LORD of hosts / will provide for all peoples / A feast of rich food and choice wines, / juicy, rich food and pure, choice wines" (Isa 25:6).

THE DAYS WILL COME

In v. 20 there is a somber shift. The expression "the day will come" is often used in the Scriptures to introduce an oracle of woe (e.g., 1 Sam 2:31; Amos 4:2; Jer 38:31; Luke 17:22; 21:6). The reference to the taking away of the bridegroom is the first allusion in Mark's Gospel to the death of Jesus. It carries an echo of Isaiah 53:8, where the suffering servant, "oppressed and condemned . . . was taken away." Most scholars doubt whether Jesus himself uttered this saying so early in his ministry. For them v. 20 reflects the post-crucifixion experience of the early church. After the death of Jesus it became appropriate for his disciples to fast.[10]

INCOMPATIBILITY OF NEW AND OLD

The parabolic sayings in vv. 21-22 bring to a climax the contrast between the new way of Jesus and the way of other religious leaders. Two illustrations involving new cloth and new wine bring home the point of the incompatibility of Jesus' new way with the old.

This is not the first time in the Gospel of Mark that the theme of newness is sounded. In Mark 1:27 the people who witness Jesus' cure of a man possessed by a demon (1:21-28) remark, "What is this? A new teaching with authority. He commands even the unclean spirits and they obey him." The word *kainos*, "new," used in 1:27 and 2:21 connotes "new in

---

[10] Other New Testament references to fasting include Matthew 6:16-18 where Jesus gives instructions on appearances when fasting. In Luke 2:27; Acts 13:2-3; 14:23 fasting accompanies prayer. In 2 Corinthians 6:5; 11:27 Paul mentions hunger among the hardships he endures for the sake of the gospel. It is unclear whether he means involuntary hunger or fasting.

quality" in contrast to *neos*, which means new chronologically, i.e., younger. In 2:22 both words are found. The new wine (*oinon neon*, i.e., new in quality) is for new wineskins (*askous kainous*, i.e., young skins). Jesus' teaching is not a younger, more contemporary version of older teaching; it is something radically new, demanding a new response.

PREACHING POSSIBILITIES

There are many directions that a preacher can follow with these parabolic sayings. One of the hardest tasks of the preacher is to discern which of these is the message that most needs to be preached at this particular time and place.

The question of the incompatibility of the new with the old is a theme that needs careful handling. A preacher must be wary of any remarks that suggest superiority of Christianity over Judaism or the replacement of the latter by the former. It is critical that Jesus always be understood as an observant Jew whose mission was directed to first-century Palestinian Jews. His first followers were Jewish who understood themselves as one of the diverse streams of pre-70 C.E. Judaism, where Pharisees, Sadducees, Essenes, Zealots, and followers of the Way all co-existed within the chosen people. There was no univocal "orthodox" Judaism in Jesus' day; there were many valid expressions of first-century Judaism. The Jesus movement most likely understood itself as a prophetic renewal movement.[11] Its focus on emancipation for those most oppressed and marginalized proved a threat to those Jewish and Roman authorities whose power was derived from systems of domination. Thus did they conspire to do away with Jesus and put an end to the momentum of his movement.

A preacher must take care not to foment Christian anti-Judaism by speaking of Christianity as a "reform movement" within Judaism. Judaism was not superseded or replaced by Christianity. Nor should Christianity be thought of as an "outgrowth" of Judaism. Rather, early Judaism and emergent

---

[11] See Elisabeth Schüssler Fiorenza, *Jesus: Miriam's Child, Sophia's Prophet* (New York: Continuum, 1994) 88–92.

Christianity were twin siblings of the same mother.[12] In their inception they were two coexisting streams of the same religion. The Gospels often retroject into the time of Jesus the later conflicts between Jews of the synagogue and those who followed Jesus. It was not until the 80s that these tensions resulted in a split between the two, when Christians were no longer welcome in the synagogue and had to choose one or the other.

It is in this context of increasing struggle for Christian self-understanding that Mark presents the Jesus movement as incompatible with emergent Pharisaic Judaism. A preacher today who chooses to focus on the theme of incompatibility must decide what will be the contrasting pole. With what is present day Christianity incompatible?

A related question that could be taken up by the preacher is the issue of Christian self-definition. How are Christians different from others? Do our practices set us visibly apart from others? What would those practices be? In a culture where comfort and self-gratification is the norm, is there an invitation in this text to a renewal of the practice of fasting on a regular basis, not only during Lent? In a culture with high consciousness of diet and weight-loss a preacher would need to articulate the motivations for fasting that are biblically based and different from these. Fasting accompanies prayer, making one more open to God and puts one in solidarity with those whose hunger is not voluntary. It can also be a sign of penitence or mourning.

The Gospel also gives an example of a process of reinterpretation of tradition in a new context that posed new questions. Verse 20 shows how the early Christians were able to theologize the adoption of a practice that differed from that of Jesus. Part of the question is timing; what was done when the earthly Jesus was alive was different from what was proper after his death. In our changed time and circumstances what traditional practices require reinterpretation?

---

[12] Alan F. Segal, *Rebecca's Children* (Cambridge: Harvard University Press, 1987); Hayim G. Perelmuter, *Siblings. Rabbinic Judaism and Early Christianity at their Beginnings* (New York: Paulist, 1989).

LECTIONARY CONTEXT

The lectionary places the Gospel in a new context, in dialogue with three other readings from the Scriptures. The first reading is intentionally chosen with a deliberate connection to the Gospel in mind. The second reading, however, is a continuous reading, usually from the Pauline literature, that may only by chance connect with the first reading and the Gospel. Oftentimes the Psalm response provides a key to understanding the juxtaposition of the other readings.[13]

The bridegroom imagery in both the first reading (Hos 2:16b, 17b, 21-22) and the Gospel invites reflection on the joy of intimate relationship with God and Christ that precedes any penitential response. In a culture that fosters self-reliance and control, a preacher can stress that fasting and other practices do not manipulate God into answering prayers in a certain way nor do they by themselves effect true repentance. Rather, God's invitation into spousal love and a believer's delight in that divine graciousness is prior. In the reading from Hosea the response God desires is a return to the whole-hearted devotion and delight of first love. The resulting bond will engender right and justice, loyal adherence to covenant fidelity, and mercy. Different from the Gospel theme, in Hosea the new is a return to the old.

If a preacher chooses to speak about the theme of God taking back faithless wife Israel, s/he must exercise great caution not to reinforce an interpretation that foments abusive patriarchal domination where the image of God as the wronged, faithful husband is misused to justify abuse of women by their husbands.

The Psalm response (Ps 103:1-2, 3-4, 8, 10, 12-13) underscores God's graciousness in dealing with sinners. The response "The Lord is kind and merciful" is well illustrated by the first reading, where God lures faithless Israel back into young love rather than cast away the adulterous spouse.

---

[13] Irene Nowell, *Sing a New Song. The Psalms in the Sunday Lectionary* (Collegeville: The Liturgical Press, 1993) 1. See also Eileen Schuller, "The Bible in the Lectionary," *Catholic Study Bible* (ed. Donald Senior; New York: Oxford, 1990) 440–51.

In the second reading (2 Cor 3:1b-6) Paul is on the defensive. Other ministers with official letters of recommendation are challenging his authority and the Torah-free Gospel he preaches. Paul, like the disciples of Jesus in the Gospel, has to justify his practices that differ from those of other religious leaders. Paul asserts that the manner of life of the Christians in Corinth makes perfectly visible the life-giving action of the Spirit in the new way he propounds. This makes further written credentials unnecessary. Paul, like Hosea and the Psalmist, points to the graciousness of God which is the source of his call to be a minister of the new covenant.

CHAPTER FIVE

Allegiances and Power

(Mark 3:20-35)

Tenth Sunday in Ordinary Time

Jesus came home with his disciples.
Again the crowd gathered,
  making it impossible for them even to eat.
When his relatives heard of this they set out to seize him,
  for they said, "He is out of his mind."
The scribes who had come from Jerusalem said,
  "He is possessed by Beelzebul,"
  and "By the prince of demons he drives out demons."

Summoning them, he began to speak to them in parables,
  "How can Satan drive out Satan?
If a kingdom is divided against itself,
  that kingdom cannot stand.
And if a house is divided against itself,
  that house will not be able to stand.
And if Satan has risen up against himself
  and is divided, he cannot stand;
  that is the end of him.
But no one can enter a strong man's house to plunder his property
  unless he first ties up the strong man.
Then he can plunder his house.
Amen, I say to you,
  all sins and all blasphemies that people utter will be
    forgiven them.
But whoever blasphemes against the Holy Spirit
  will never have forgiveness,
  but is guilty of an everlasting sin."
For they had said, "He has an unclean spirit."
His mother and his brothers arrived.
Standing outside they sent word to him and called him.

A crowd seated around him told him,
  "Your mother and your brothers and your sisters
  are outside asking for you."
But he said to them in reply,
  "Who are my mother and my brothers?"
And looking around at those seated in the circle he said,
  "Here are my mother and my brothers.
For whoever does the will of God
  is my brother and sister and mother."

MARCAN LITERARY CONTEXT

This passage comes on the heels of Jesus' choice of the Twelve (Mark 3:13-19) and precedes the major complex of parables in Mark 4:1-34. Mark has narrated both positive and negative responses to the beginning of Jesus' public ministry. On the one hand Mark depicts a series of five episodes in which Jesus stands in conflict with the scribes and the Pharisees (2:1–3:6). On the other hand, he also shows people "from Jerusalem, from Idumea, from beyond the Jordan, and from the neighborhood of Tyre and Sidon" (3:8) flocking to Jesus for healing. In the Gospel assigned for this Sunday conflict surfaces again. But this time the challengers are not only the scribes, but Jesus' own relatives.

This section of the Gospel has a clearly chiastic literary structure:[1]

A. The family of Jesus seeks him	3:20-21
B. First Accusation: He is possessed by Beelzebul	3:22a
C. Second Accusation: His power is from the prince of demons	3:22b
D. Sayings about Satan and Divided Power	3:23-26
C.' Response to Second Accusation	3:27
B.' Response to First Accusation	3:28-30
A.' The true family of Jesus	3:31-35

Mark often uses a technique of framing important episodes, as he does here. The conflict with Jesus' family (3:20-21) and the delineation of his true family (3:31-35) bracket the key parabolic sayings about Satan and divided power.

---

[1] Harrington, *Mark*, 43.

FAMILY CONFLICT (3:20-21, 31-35)

The passage opens with the statement, "He came home with his disciples" (v. 20). Whereas Mark 6:1 informs us that Jesus' native place is Nazareth, it becomes clear from 3:21 that "home" in 3:20 is not where Jesus' relatives are. The evangelist opens his second chapter by saying, "When Jesus returned to Capernaum after some days, it became known that he was at home" (2:1). According to Mark this town was also the home of Simon and Andrew and is the place of Jesus' first healings. The evangelist gives the impression that Jesus has made the village of Capernaum his home base for his Galilean ministry.

In v. 21 Jesus' family[2] sets out to seize him. In the wider context of Mark's Gospel this is far from a friendly action. The other instances of the verb *krateō* ("to seize") refer to the arrests of John the Baptist (6:17) and Jesus (12:12; 14:1, 44, 46, 49, 51). Their motive for seizing Jesus is that he is "out of his mind" (*exestē*, literally, "beside himself"). It is unclear from the third person plural verb *elegon*, "they were saying," whether the subject is Jesus' relatives or other people.

Social-science criticism sheds light on what is the perceived threat to Jesus' family. In Jesus' first-century Palestinian world a family's honor is its most prized possession. People gain and keep honor by two means: it is ascribed by birth or inheritance or acquired through interactions that are public. The latter depends on the response from others and public perception of the exchange.[3] As Mark describes this incident, Jesus' family is concerned that what he is doing will detract from their public good name.

It is also important to understand the concept of dyadic personality that underlies the self-understanding of a person of Jesus' world. In contrast to contemporary Western culture's

---

[2] The Greek phrase *hoi par' autou* (literally, "those around him") can include neighbors and friends as well as family and relatives.

[3] See Bruce Malina, *The New Testament World. Insights from Cultural Anthropology,* rev. ed. (Louisville: Westminster John Knox, 1993); Bruce J. Malina and Richard L. Rohrbaugh, *Social Science Commentary on the Synoptic Gospels* (Minneapolis: Fortress, 1992); John J. Pilch, *The Cultural World of Jesus. Sunday by Sunday, Cycle B* (Collegeville: The Liturgical Press, 1996); David M. May, "Mark 3:20-35 from the Perspective of Shame/Honor," *BTB* 17 (1987) 83–87.

emphasis on rugged individualism, a person in Jesus' day lived always in the context of the groups to which they belonged. Their self-definition would always be given in terms of their family and clan relationships, their village context, and their religious group. A good example is Paul's self-definition in Phil 3:5, ". . . of the race of Israel, of the tribe of Benjamin, a Hebrew of Hebrew parentage, in observance of the law a Pharisee." Another is Mark 6:3, where those who hear Jesus teach in his hometown synagogue are mystified by his words. They ask, "Is he not the carpenter, the son of Mary, and the brother of James and Joses and Judas and Simon? And are not his sisters here with us?" In Jesus' world life is lived imbedded in one's family context.

THE NEW FAMILY

There is no parallel in Matthew or Luke for the opening verses of Mark 3:20-21. In the other two Synoptic Gospels the Infancy Narratives show that Jesus' family[4] does have knowledge about his mission. However, all three recount the episode in which Jesus defines his family as those who do the will of God (Mark 3:30-35 // Matt 12:46-50 // Luke 8:19-21). Throughout Mark's Gospel there is a sharp distinction drawn between insiders and outsiders, that is, those who hear Jesus and respond positively, and those who refuse to follow him. Mark paints a harsh portrait[5] of Jesus' natural family, who stands "outside" (v. 31) while a crowd sits around him (v. 32).

---

[4] The mention of Jesus' brothers and sisters in this passage raises questions in light of the doctrine of Mary's perpetual virginity. First, a clarification about terminology is in order, as there are differences in English translations. The Greek text in vv. 31, 33, 34 has the masculine plural *adelphoi*, which can denote both brothers and sisters. In v. 32 many early Greek manuscripts add *kai hai adelphai sou*, "and your sisters." Verse 35 lists separately "brother and sister and mother." For a detailed study of the history of interpretation regarding the sisters and brothers of Jesus, see John P. Meier, *A Marginal Jew. Rethinking the Historical Jesus* (ABRL; vol. 1; New York: Doubleday, 1991) 318–32. He outlines various solutions, e.g., that the "brothers" were really cousins or stepbrothers of Jesus. Meier concludes on the basis of multiple attestation, philological analysis, and historical probability that the brothers and sisters of Jesus were his siblings.

[5] Luke's version (8:19-21) allows that Jesus' family may be among those who hear the word of God and do it. He paints a very positive portrait of

To people of Jesus' world whose family is the source of status and is the primary economic, religious, educational, and social matrix, Jesus' response to his mother and siblings is shocking. To lose one's connection to family meant the loss of vital networks,[6] creating a threat to one's very existence. Survival would depend on attachment to a new group, a surrogate family. Later in the Gospel Jesus assures his disciples that those who abandon their family of origin for the Christian family would reap rewards of one hundred fold in the present age and eternal life in the age to come (Mark 10:30). Jesus defines his family not as those with whom he shares blood relation, but rather those who share his commitment to do the will of God.

From the perspective of honor and shame, Jesus' family avoids dishonor by not directly confronting him publicly over a family dispute; to do so would be shameful.[7] Jesus' response places God's honor above that of his family. The result is that Jesus is portrayed not as dishonoring his family, but as achieving even higher honor by devoting himself to the honor of God.[8]

POSSESSED BY BEELZEBUL

In vv. 22-30 the focus of conflict shifts. Now the antagonists are scribes, who are cast in opposition to Jesus throughout the Gospel of Mark. At the outset of his ministry Jesus' authoritative teaching is contrasted with that of the scribes (1:22). The scribes figure twice in the first complex of conflict stories (2:6, 16). They continue to play the role of foil to Jesus and play a prominent part in the passion narrative.[9] One exception is 12:28-34 where Jesus declares that a scribe who asks him about the greatest commandment is not far from the reign of God.

Mary in his infancy narratives, and although she does not appear as a disciple of Jesus in the rest of the Gospel, Luke places her and Jesus' siblings with the disciples in the upper room awaiting the coming of the Spirit in Acts 1:14.

6 Malina and Rohrbaugh, *Social Science Commentary*, 201.

7 May, "Shame/Honor," 86.

8 Ibid., 86.

9 Mark 7:1, 5; 8:31; 9:11, 14; 10:33; 11:18, 27; 12:35, 38; 14:1, 43, 53; 15:1, 31.

There are two accusations put forth by the scribes: Jesus is possessed by Beelzebul,[10] and the source of his power of exorcism is the prince of demons. Such a public accusation is very serious. Unless Jesus can successfully refute it his ministerial career could be ruined. Jesus counters the charges in several steps, using parables.[11] First Jesus points out the absurdity of the scribes' accusation. He shifts to the term "Satan," a name with a varied history. In the Hebrew Scriptures "satan" refers usually to a human being who is an "accuser" or "adversary." In later development, Satan became a proper name for the leader of evil forces. In the New Testament Satan is synonymous with "the devil" (e.g., Matt 4:1-8), "the evil one" (e.g., Matt 13:19), and "the ruler of this world" (John 14:30).[12]

Prior to this Gospel episode Mark has shown Jesus tempted by Satan in the desert, but able to resist with the aid of ministrations of angels (1:13). He has also recounted that Jesus cured people possessed by demons[13] (1:21-28, 32, 39; 3:11) and that he gave his followers authority to do the same (3:15). Later in the Gospel Jesus rebukes Peter as "Satan" when he rejects Jesus' saying about his coming passion (8:33). In the narrative logic of the Gospel, Jesus is clearly not Satan. Jesus' retort to the scribes shows how ludicrous is their accusation: if he were Satan, how could he be casting out his own self? (v. 23). Two maxims (vv. 24-25) in parallel construction reinforce this. No kingdom or house divided is able to stand. If, in fact, Satan is divided against himself his end is in view (v. 26).

---

[10] For possible etymologies of the name Beelzebul see Theodore J. Lewis, "Beelzebul," *ABD* I. 638–39.

[11] Malina and Rohrbaugh, *Social Science Commentary*, 200–01.

[12] See Betty Jane Lillie, Patricia M. McDonald, and Robert J. Schreiter, "Satan," *The Collegeville Pastoral Dictionary of Biblical Theology* (ed. Carroll Stuhlmueller; Collegeville: The Liturgical Press, 1996) 874–79.

[13] In antiquity many varieties of illness were labeled "demon possession." Today these would be recognized as mental disorders or would be attributed to other physical causes.

BINDING THE STRONG MAN

There is a foreshadowing in v. 26 of the end of the reign of evil. It is not because of civil war, however, that Satan will be defeated, but by the inbreaking of the reign of God, culminating in the death and resurrection of Jesus.[14] The parabolic saying in v. 27 completes the thought: in order for the "strong man," Satan, to be robbed of his power, another must bind him.[15] Mark has already designated Jesus as the stronger one, when John the Baptist proclaimed, "One mightier than I is coming after me" (1:7). Jesus' exorcisms are evidence that Satan's house has already been broken into and his possessions are being dissipated.

BLASPHEMY AGAINST THE HOLY SPIRIT

Having refuted the accusation of using the power of the prince of demons, Jesus rebuts the charge of possession by an unclean spirit (vv. 28-30). There has been much speculation over the meaning of the saying in v. 29 about the one unforgivable sin, "blasphemy." Verse 29 seems to contradict v. 28 where Jesus asserts that forgiveness is possible for all sins. It also seems to go against the grain of the whole fabric of Jesus' life of forgiving love. According to Luke, Jesus even forgave those who put him to death (23:34) and he taught his followers to forgive a limitless number of offenses (Matt 18:22; Luke 17:4).

Some scholars resolve the difficulty by understanding vv. 28-29 as two sides of an early Christian debate. The question behind the text may have been whether those Christians who under threat of persecution have apostasized ("blasphemed") can be forgiven. Mark's community may have wrestled with whether or not to welcome back repentant members who had foresworn Christ and had betrayed the community. Could such a one be trusted again? In such a scenario, v. 28 reflects

---

[14] Luke 22:3 and John 13:27 are more explicit about the role of Satan in the passion of Jesus.

[15] The saying may have been inspired by Isaiah 49:24-25, "Thus says the LORD: Can booty be taken from a warrior? or captives be rescued from a tyrant? Yes, captives can be taken from a warrior, and booty be rescued from a tyrant; Those who oppose you I will oppose, and your sons I will save."

the position of those who say "yes"; v. 29 that of those who say "no."[16] An alternative solution is that v. 28 reflects the words of Jesus, who advocated unlimited forgiveness; in v. 29 is a qualification added by the early Church.

Whether or not this historical reconstruction is correct, the literary context gives another meaning to the sayings. They are Jesus' response to the scribes who attribute Jesus' power to the prince of demons rather than to the holy Spirit. These religious leaders who claim to know the workings of God neither recognize that the reign of God has come in the person of Jesus (Mark 1:14-15) nor that the Spirit is the driving force behind his ministry (Mark 1:8, 10, 12). The debate with the scribes ends with Jesus making a counter-accusation against his opponents: they blaspheme against the holy Spirit. Their silence is tantamount to acquiescencing to the charge and signals a victory for Jesus. The irony in Mark's Gospel is that the very charge of blasphemy is hurled at Jesus by the high priest in the passion narrative (14:64).

PREACHING POSSIBILITIES

This Gospel presents both peril and possibility. Two separate conflicts with two different sets of opponents invite the listeners to examine their stances and presuppositions. Where is the true power of the Spirit evident? And with whom are disciples' primary allegiances?

The two questions are not unrelated, as Mark's chiastic structure underscores. With regard to the question of power, a Christian must wrestle with identifying what are the contemporary manifestations of the power of Jesus. Where is the liberating power of the Spirit at work today in releasing from their bonds those who are most downtrodden? How is Christ's power manifest in dismantling systems of injustice and domination? Where must Christians position themselves both individually and communally in order to loose the fetters of racism,

---

[16] Such a technique, of placing two differing opinions side by side is common in rabbinic literature. Two oft-quoted figures from the late first century B.C.E. were Rabbi Hillel, who commonly responded affirmatively to questions that received a negative response from the more conservative Rabbi Shammai.

sexism, classism, ageism, militarism, etc. to continue Jesus' work
of bringing to an end the rule of evil powers?

The Gospel also raises the question: what revilement and
accusations are Christians willing to endure if they challenge
the ruling powers? In Mark 13:11 Jesus assures his followers
that when they are persecuted and handed over to the authorities they are not to worry. He says, "When they lead you away
and hand you over, do not worry beforehand about what you
are to say. But say whatever will be given to you at that hour.
For it will not be you who are speaking but the holy Spirit." In
light of this passage "blasphemy against the holy Spirit" would
be a rejection of the promptings of the Spirit when one is under
duress and a denial of the saving power of Jesus' way of forgiving love.

There is great hope offered in the promise of ever-possible
forgiveness. Only when one refuses to be open to the power of
God is forgiveness denied. Only deliberate refusal to recognize the power of the Spirit cuts one off from God's graciousness. God's offer is always present and available.

The Gospel also opens up sobering questions about Christian allegiances. Commitment to the Gospel can call into question not only one's ties with powers that reinforce domination,
but also with family members, as well as friends, coworkers,
and community members. Conflicts can arise from differing expressions of faith commitments, differing interpretations of the
Gospel, and differing ideas about the demands of discipleship.
Just as Jesus experienced, and even provoked, such conflict, disciples today should also expect it. No one, however, is left to
face these struggles alone. Disciples have networks of support
within the community of believers. Followers of Jesus may be
required, for the sake of the Gospel, to put their allegiance to
this new family of believers above ties to their family of origin.

It is also notable that in this Gospel pericope the tactic for
discrediting Jesus is name-calling and labeling. While in Jesus'
day this was a strategy for honoring or shaming, today we
might reflect on the use of epithets to stereotype and dismiss
people. In Mark 3:21-30 Jesus does not imitate his detractors
by name-calling. Naming evil is different from name-calling.
Jesus names his opponents' distorted logic and their mistaken

evaluation of his deeds. But he does so by posing pointed questions (v. 23), pronouncing true maxims (vv. 24-27), and presenting an invitation to forgiveness (vv. 28-29). He does not label the scribes in a way that would lock them into their false positions. Rather, his responses leave open the door for them to be persuaded to his way. This passage provides Christians an opportunity to reflect on how we speak of and to those with whom we disagree. Can a parabolic response provide a better way toward conversion and transformation?

Finally, this Gospel does not deny that Satan or powers of evil exist. A Christian recognizes that the reign of God has not yet arrived in its fullness. But believers can already claim the overwhelming victory that Christ has won over evil and sin.

LECTIONARY CONTEXT

While the Gospel focuses on correct identification of Jesus' power over the forces of evil, the first reading from Genesis 3:9-15 tells in mythological form the origin of suffering and evil and division in the world. According to Genesis these were not intended by God at creation, but entered the world as a consequence of human disobedience. Both the woman and man acted against God's directives; both are held accountable. The narrative depicts the resulting division: the human beings become afraid and hide from God. The man blames the woman for their difficulties and the woman blames the serpent. Separation and enmity now enter the world where there was previously harmonious coexistence.

The responsorial psalm (Ps 130:1-2, 3-4, 5-6, 7-8), like v. 28 in the Gospel, allays fearfulness in the face of sin and evil: "With the Lord there is mercy, and fullness of redemption." There is no hope if God adds up our dalliances with evil. Redemption is assured, though, to those who trust in God's boundless loving kindness and forgiveness.

Paul's letter to the Corinthians (2 Cor 4:13–5:1) echoes this same confidence that God will bestow abundant grace on those who trust in God's power. The one who raised Jesus from the dead is able also to raise us to new life, even if present trials and tribulations make God's power over evil difficult to discern now.

CHAPTER SIX

Gradual Growth
and Mischievous Mustard
(Mark 4:26-34)

Eleventh Sunday of Ordinary Time

Jesus said to the crowds:
"This is how it is with the kingdom of God;
it is as if a man were to scatter seed on the land
and would sleep and rise night and day
and through it all the seed would sprout and grow,
he knows not how.
Of its own accord the land yields fruit,
first the blade, then the ear, then the full grain in the ear.
And when the grain is ripe, he wields the sickle at once,
for the harvest has come."

He said,
"To what shall we compare the kingdom of God,
or what parable can we use for it?
It is like a mustard seed that, when it is sown in the ground,
is the smallest of all the seeds on the earth.
But once it is sown, it springs up and becomes the largest of plants
and puts forth large branches,
so that the birds of the sky can dwell in its shade."
With many such parables
he spoke the word to them as they were able to understand it.
Without parables he did not speak to them,
but to his own disciples he explained everything in private.

MARCAN LITERARY CONTEXT

The first three chapters of Mark focus on the healing and exorcisms performed by Jesus at the outset of his Galilean ministry.
These deeds of power provoke both positive and negative

responses. Some are moved to follow Jesus as his disciples; others reject him and even begin to plot his death (3:6). In chapter 4 the focus is on Jesus as teacher. In this chapter are clustered the majority of the Marcan parables. Undoubtedly these had already been collected together in a pre-Marcan source. Like Jesus' healings, his parables also have a mixed reception.

Most scholars see a chiastic or concentric structure to Mark 4, although there is some disagreement as to which parable or sayings stand at the center. Some delineate it thus:[1]

A. Introduction	4:1-2
B. Sower Parable	4:3-9
C. Reason for Speaking in Parables	4:10-12
D. Allegory of Seeds	4:13-20
C.' Enigmatic Sayings	4:21-25
B.' Seed Parables	4:26-32
A.' Conclusion	4:33-34

In this structure the explanation of the parable is central and introduces one of Mark's primary themes: the incomprehension of the disciples. Others put the sayings in vv. 21-25 at the center:[2]

A. Introduction	4:1-2a
B. Parable Material	4:2b-20
C. Sayings Material	4:21-25
B.' Parable Material	4:26-32
A.' Conclusion	4:33-34

In this outline, the enigmatic sayings stand at the center and underscore the paradoxical dual purpose of the parables that both reveal and confound.

---

[1] John R. Donahue, *The Gospel in Parable* (Philadelphia: Fortress, 1988) 31; G.Fay, "Introduction to Incomprehension: The Literary Structure of Mark 4:1-34," *CBQ* 51 (1989) 65–81; Elian Cuvillier, *Le concept de παραβολή dans le second évangile* (EB n.s. 19; Paris: Gabalda, 1993) 117; Joel Marcus, *The Mystery of the Kingdom of God* (SBLDS 90; Atlanta: Scholars Press, 1986) 221. Bas van Iersel (*Reading Mark* [Collegeville: The Liturgical Press, 1988] 70) combines this structure and the next by placing 4:10-25 at the center.

[2] Augustine Stock, *The Method and Message of Mark* (Wilmington, Del.: Glazier, 1989) 164; Jan Lambrecht, *Once More Astonished. The Parables of Jesus* (New York: Crossroad, 1981) 86–87; Joanna Dewey, *Marcan Public Debate* (SBLDS 48; Chico, Calif.: Scholars, 1980) 147–52.

Another way of delineating the chapter sees it not as chiastic but divided in two parts: 4:1-23 and 4:24-34.[3] The first part weaves together three elements:

1. The Sower Parable (4:4-8) and its explanation (4:13-20)
2. Mark's reflection on the paradoxical nature of parable discourse: as mystery to be obscured (4:10-12) but also as secret to be revealed (4:21-22)
3. The thematic refrain of listening (4:3, 9, 23)

The second part interlocks with vv. 21-23 thus:[4]

a   And he said to them, (v. 21a)
   b   Is a lamp brought in to be put under a bushel . . . (v. 21b)
     c   For there is nothing hid (v. 22a)
       d   If anyone has ears to hear let them hear (v. 23)
a' And he said to them, (v. 24a)
       d' Beware what you hear (v. 24b)
   b' The measure you give is the measure you get . . . (v. 24c)
     c' For to the one who has . . . (v. 25)

In this pattern the structure of the sayings is seen as similar (a = introduction, b = statement, c = corollary), held together by catch themes of listening (d) and "measuring" (b; "bushel" is a unit of measurement).

Each way of delineating the chapter places the emphasis slightly differently. In whichever structure one adopts, the parables that appear in the Gospel passage for this Sunday are the conclusion of a larger parable complex. The other parables of Mark 4 do not appear in the Sunday lectionary, but are assigned to Week 3 of Ordinary Time. The section for this Sunday, Mark 4:26-34 consists of two separate parables (vv. 26-29 and vv. 30-32) and concluding sayings (vv. 33-34) about Jesus' habitual teaching in parables and their intelligibility or lack thereof.

GRADUAL GROWTH, SLEEPY SOWER, OR HURRIED HARVESTER? (Mark 4:26-29)

This little parable is found only in Mark. It is linked to the first parable in Mark 4 by the common themes of sowing and harvesting. This is the first Marcan parable that is explicitly

---

[3] Ched Myers, *Binding The Strong Man* (Maryknoll, N.Y.: Orbis, 1988) 170–71.
[4] Ibid., 170–71.

about the reign of God (v. 26). But what, exactly, is its point? Is
the focus on the sower, the process of growth of the seed, or
the harvest? A case can be made for each of these.[5]
Some scholars see the sower at the center of the parable.[6] He
is introduced immediately in v. 26 and it is his actions of scattering seed, sleeping, rising, and not knowing that dominate the
first two verses. In v. 28 the subject shifts to the earth and its productive activity, but v. 29 returns to the action of the farmer. But
then the question arises, who does the farmer represent?

THE SOWER AS GOD

One possibility is that the sower stands for God, who is
active in bringing the divine realm to fruition even if this remains imperceptible to humans. That the sower represents
God is supported by the allusion in Mark 4:29 to Joel 4:13,
"Apply the sickle, / for the harvest is ripe; / Come and tread,
/ for the wine press is full; / The vats overflow, / for great is
their malice." In Joel the harvesting metaphor connotes God's
visitation of punishment upon the nations for their crimes.

Two difficulties with understanding the sower as God in
Mark 4:26-29 are the references to sleeping and to not knowing
in v. 27. In response to the first objection, God's "sleeping" can
be understood as human perception that God seems removed
from human pleas or concerns. Similar references to God's apparent inactivity toward the covenant people are found in the
Hebrew Scriptures. At times God seems silent (e.g., Pss 22:2;
35:22), or hidden (Ps 13:1; Isa 59:2), or apparently needs to be
awakened to the peoples' pleas (Pss 35:23; 44:23).

The second difficulty, however, has not been satisfactorily
resolved. How can it be that God does not know how the seed
sprouts and grows (v. 27)? Some commentators try to resolve
the problem by translating v. 27c: "And he gives the impression
of being uninterested in what is happening."[7] This translation
adds a nuance that is not entirely faithful to the original text.

---

[5] See Joel Marcus, *The Mystery of the Kingdom of God* (SBLDS 90; Atlanta:
Scholars Press, 1986) 163–200.

[6] Ibid.

[7] J. Dupont, "La parabole de la semence qui pousse toute seule (Marc
4,26-29)," *RSR* 55 (1979) 381–83.

DISCIPLES AS SOWERS

Another possibility is that the sower represents a Christian disciple, who goes about the work of evangelization, not always comprehending, but allowing God's action to bring it to fullness. From this angle the "not knowing" is quite coherent with Mark's depiction of the disciples. The theme of their lack of understanding[8] sounds for the first time in Mark 4:13 and resurfaces in 8:17-21, 33; 9:32; 10:38. There is also a connection between Mark 4:26-29 and the Gethsemane scene (14:32-42), where sleeping and rising and incomprehension of the disciples converge. Some scholars[9] see a link between Mark 4:26-29 and other late-first-century Jewish literature such as 4 Ezra 4:26-43 and *2 Apoc. Bar.* 22:5-7; 23:2 in which the theme is also found of disciples not knowing when the end time will come ("harvest" frequently stands for the end time).[10]

A difficulty with this interpretation, however, is that elsewhere in Mark the disciples' incomprehension is cause for rebuke from Jesus. In 4:26-29 this element does not fit. Moreover, the assignation of the part of harvester to the disciples (v. 29) is unique. This role is always assigned to God or Christ.

JESUS AS SOWER

A third possibility is that the sower represents Jesus. The seed that he scatters (as in Mark 4:14) is the word. In its original setting this could be a parable of reassurance that despite present appearances his preaching will bear a good harvest. His sleeping and rising has echoes in the subsequent episode

---

[8] On this theme see Ernest Best, *Following Jesus: Discipleship in the Gospel of Mark* (JSNTS 4; Sheffield: JSOT, 1981; Dennis Sweetland, *Our Journey with Jesus: Discipleship According to Mark* (GNS 22; Wilmington, Del.: Glazier, 1987); D. J. Hawkins, "The Incomprehension of the Disciples in the Markan Redaction," *JBL* 91 (1972) 491–500; Elizabeth Struthers Malbon, "Fallible Followers: Women and Men in the Gospel of Mark," *Semeia* 28 (1983) 29–48; Robert C. Tannehill, "The Disciples in Mark: The Function of a Narrative Role," *JR* 57 (1977) 386–405; Joseph B. Tyson, "The Blindness of the Disciples in Mark," *JBL* 80 (1961) 261–68.

[9] E.g., Marcus, *Mystery*, 174.

[10] E.g., Matthew 13:30, 39; 21:34, 41; John 4:35-36; Galatians 6:9; Revelation 14:15.

(Mark 4:35-41) where Jesus' disciples rouse him during a frightful storm. This may also be an allusion to Jesus' death and resurrection (as in 1 Thess 5:10; Eph 5:14).

In the setting of Mark's community the parable may reflect their experience that Jesus seems absent to them during their time of present suffering while they await the parousia. The parable offers assurance that the process of growth toward the end time is proceeding according to God's plan. That Jesus does not know the timing of the end is not problematic in light of Mark 13:32, "But of that day or hour, no one knows, neither the angels in heaven, nor the Son, but only the Father." Nor is there a difficulty in casting Jesus in a role of end-time harvester. Mark 13:27 presents a similar image where Jesus says that the Human One "will send out the angels and gather [his] elect from the four winds, from the end of the earth to the end of the sky."[11]

HOW THE SEED GROWS

Other interpretations focus not on the identity of the sower, but on the manner of growth of the seed. In its original context the parable may have been directed toward certain Pharisees, for whom greater human observance of the Law could hasten the coming of the messianic kingdom. Or perhaps it was aimed at those who had affinity with the Zealots,[12] who advocated that God's reign would be accomplished by taking up arms against the Romans. The parable, then, advocates patience and asserts that the reign of God is God's doing according to God's timing, and is not dependent on human action.[13] One way to read Mark 4:26-29 is that the sower does nothing more than plant the seed; after that nothing is narrated about further work by the farmer.[14] The earth produces automatically (*automatē*,

---

[11]   Similarly Matthew 13:41; John 5:27; Revelation 14:15.

[12]   This has been proposed by a number of commentators. See Dupont, "La parabole," 375 n. 28 for references.

[13]   E.g., Raymond Collins, "The Story of a Seed Growing by Itself. A Parable for our Times," *Emmanuel* 94 (1988) 446–52; Joachim Jeremias, *The Parables of Jesus* (rev. ed.; New York: Scribner's Sons, 1972) 151–53.

[14]   John Paul Heil, "Reader-Response and the Narrative Context of the Parables about Growing Seed in Mark 4:1-34," *CBQ* 54 (1992) 282–83; Eugene

v. 28); the sower does not know how (v. 27). A similar motif is found in Paul's insistence, "I planted, Apollos watered, but God caused the growth. Therefore, neither the one who plants nor the one who waters is anything, but only God, who causes the growth" (1 Cor 3:6-7).

READINESS FOR THE HARVEST

One other possibility is that the emphasis of the parable is neither on the seed nor the sower, but on readiness for the harvest.[15] Attending to the narrative dynamics, the parable climaxes with the harvest that brings to fulfillment all the actions of the sower. The farmer may not know how the seed sprouts and grows (v. 27), but he certainly is not idle. He goes about his normal routines: scattering seed, sleeping and rising.[16] The growth of the seed is not secret; the sower monitors its production first of the blade, then the ear, then the full grain in the ear. The emphasis falls on the farmer's ability to recognize the critical moment when the grain is ripe and at once the harvest must be reaped. This is the moment when God's time and human time intersect, when tranquil human rhythms are disrupted by the full manifestation of God's power and there is a call for immediate response.[17]

MISCHIEVOUS MUSTARD (4:30-32)

In Mark's Gospel the parable of the mustard seed is paired with the parable of the growing seed. Matthew (13:31-33) and Luke (13:18-21) link the mustard seed parable with that of the woman mixing yeast in bread dough, a parable that Mark lacks. A version of the mustard seed parable is also found in

---

LaVerdiere, "Teaching in Parables," *Emmanuel* 94 (1988) 453; Douglas Oakman, *Jesus and the Economic Questions of His Day* (SBEC 8; Lewiston/Queenston: Mellen, 1986) 110–14; Marie Sabin, "Reading Mark 4 as Midrash," *JSNT* 45 (1992) 16.

[15] Claude N. Pavur, "The Grain is Ripe: Parabolic Meaning in Mark 4:26-29," *BTB* 17 (1987) 21–23.

[16] The sequence of sleeping and rising, night and day reflects a Jewish reckoning of the day from sundown to sundown.

[17] Donahue, *The Gospel in Parable*, 34–36.

Gos.Thom. §20, not connected with either of the other two parables. It is evident that the parable originally circulated independently and became joined to the parable of the growing seed by the verbal connections "kingdom of God" and "seed." At first blush, the parable appears to be one of contrast: tiny mustard seed grows into the greatest of all shrubs. Botanically speaking mustard does not grow to be the greatest of all shrubs, nor is it the smallest of all seeds; hyperbole is used to drive home the contrast. However, mustard seed was proverbial for its tiny size, as Jesus' saying to his disciples in Matthew 17:20 (// Luke 17:6) shows, "Amen, I say to you, if you have faith the size of a mustard seed, you will say to this mountain, 'Move from here to there,' and it will move. Nothing will be impossible for you."

For some scholars Jesus spoke this parable to his discouraged disciples to reassure them that although his ministry did not seem to amount to much at the outset, there would come a time when he would have a huge, universal following. This interpretation of the slow, but inevitable growth of the Church as the locus of the reign of God was most popular in the nineteenth century with the rise of evolutionary science.

The detail of the sheltering tree has been interpreted in light of several passages from the Hebrew Scriptures where a tree with nesting birds symbolizes a powerful nation gathering other peoples under its sway. In Daniel 4:7-9 the strong tree whose top touched the heavens and in whose branches the birds of the air nested represents the power of Nebuchadnezzar, king of Babylon, whose rule extended over the whole earth (Dan 4:19). Similar imagery is found in Ezekiel 17:22-24, where Yhwh plants a cedar shoot atop the mountain heights of Israel. It becomes a majestic tree beneath which birds of every kind shall dwell. The prophecy envisions the end-time gathering in of all the Gentile nations, like nesting birds, under the sheltering embrace of Israel. In light of these passages, commentators have understood Jesus' parable of the mighty mustard with its nesting birds to point toward the end-time when all will be drawn into the bosom of the Christian way.

More recently, scholars have followed the lead of Robert Funk, who proposed that the parable is really a burlesque of

Ezekiel's cedar figure with a comic twist.[18] He proposes that Jesus' parable is meant to contrast mustard, the common garden weed, with cedar, the most majestic tree, as an image of God's reign. The reign of God does not have to be imported from far-away Lebanon, nor does it come with an impressive power. Rather, it is found in every back yard, erupting out of unpretentious ventures of faith by unimportant people—but which have potentially world-transforming power!

Furthermore, wild mustard, often regarded as a pesky weed, is impossible to eradicate once it has infested a field.[19] So too is the tenacious faith of those who seem to be of no account. From this perspective another point emerges: the reign of God, like wild mustard that menaces the cultivated field, is a threat to the upper classes who live off the toil of the poor cultivator.[20] Not only is the mustard dangerous, but also the needy birds it attracts, who can also be destructive to the crop. The weed-like reign of God poses a challenge to the arrangements of civilization and those who benefit from them. This interpretation poses a disturbing challenge to the hearer: Where is God's reign to be found? With what kind of power is it established? Who brings it? Who stands to gain by its coming? Whose power is threatened by it?

INSIDE / OUTSIDE (4:33-34)

The final two verses of this passage are the conclusion of the whole complex of parables in Mark 4 and they complete the framework opened with vv. 1-2. The first phrase of both vv. 33 and 34 recapitulate v. 2, "he taught them at length in parables." There is some debate as to the meaning of the second halves of vv. 33 and 34. Is v. 33b, "as they were able to understand it," to be understood in a positive way, i.e., that Jesus adapted himself to the capabilities of his audience? Taken in isolation, that meaning would be logical. However, in its

---

[18] Robert Funk, "The Looking Glass Tree is for the Birds," *Int* 27 (1973) 3–9.

[19] Oakman, *Economic Questions*, 125. See Pliny the Elder, *Natural History* 19.171, who distinguishes three kinds of mustard and describes the uncontrollable growth of wild mustard.

[20] Oakman, *Economic Questions*, 127–28.

present context it is more likely that v. 33b should be interpreted in a more restrictive sense, i.e., "only in the way they could understand."[21]

In Mark 4:10-12 the disciples have already raised the question of how they are to understand Jesus' parables. Jesus uses the words of Isaiah (6:9) to draw a line between insiders and outsiders (4:12), a theme that also comes to the fore in the episode with his family in 3:31-34. Mark 4:33-34 reiterates what is asserted in Mark 4:11-12: parables are enigmatic speech that cannot be understood by those who have chosen to remain on the outside. But to those who choose to follow Jesus the mystery is gradually unfolded for them. One must decide whether to place oneself inside the circle "around [Jesus]" (4:1, 10) or whether to stand with the unperceiving outsiders.

PREACHING POSSIBILITIES

Both parables in this Gospel present a number of preaching possibilities. The preacher would do well to focus on only one main point. One of the tasks of the preacher is to discern which of the many possible points is the one that needs to be preached at this time and place. In another moment and place the choice might be very different.

One aspect of the first parable worth consideration is the point that God is the source of all productivity.[22] In a culture where people find themselves caught in the webs of overwork, where increased productivity and increased profit are the supreme goals, the parable of the growing seed could offer an invitation to recognize God's grace that does not depend on human efforts. This parable could point toward a renewal of sabbath observance, by which a disciple's life can be lived by a more balanced rhythm of sleeping and rising, working and resting. In this way, believers glorify God by performing the productive work of the sower, but recognize that the growth of the seed ultimately depends on God.

Another variation of this theme is that the parable of the growing seed, when addressed to poor people who labor

---

21 Lambrecht, *Once More Astonished*, 91.
22 Collins, "The Story of a Seed," 451.

mightily in the employ of others for bare subsistence, may offer a vision of eschatological rest. Like the sower who does nothing to bring about the harvest, so too will there be no more back-breaking toil for poor laborers in the fullness of God's realm.[23] Another direction the preacher can take from the first parable is to emphasize the necessity of living the rhythms of Christian life so as to be ready for the decisive end-time moment, whether that be the end of one's own life, or the parousia. A farmer cannot reap a good harvest if there has never been any seed sown or tended.

The preacher might also focus on assurance that God is at work, even when the divine action seems imperceptible or unintelligible. In its original setting the parable of the growing seed may have assured followers of Jesus that the word he preached would eventually bear a good harvest, even if the beginnings seemed very modest.[24] Likewise, the parable of the mustard seed can be one that assures disciples that inauspicious beginnings can end with grand results.

From the mustard parable the preacher could also choose to focus on the locale of the reign of God and its manner of coming. It is not imported from far off, but comes with every small venture of faith by ordinary believers who act in the power of the crucified and risen Christ. Such ventures pose a challenge to oppressive systems of power just as mustard run wild can overtake cultivated fields. These kinds of efforts also shelter the little ones who, like the birds of the air depend on God's benefaction for existence (Luke 12:24). This subversive power of radical faith, like mustard gone to seed, is impossible to root out once it has taken hold.

The final verses of the Gospel urge the preacher to make clear how important is the challenge that faces the hearer of these parables. They are not peaceful stories about birds and plants and rhythms of nature. Rather, they pose difficult challenges and invitations to conversion. The choice must be made whether to be included with the "insiders" who struggle to

---

[23] Oakman, *Economic Questions*, 110–14.

[24] Herman Hendrickx, *The Parables of Jesus*, rev. ed. (San Francisco: Harper & Row, 1986) 40; LaVerdiere, "Teaching in Parables," 453.

understand and follow Jesus, or whether to stand outside looking but not seeing, hearing but not listening (4:12).

LECTIONARY CONTEXT

The first reading from Ezekiel 17:22-24 speaks of a tender shoot that God will take from the powerful cedar and plant on the mountain heights of Israel. This is a metaphor for the remnant of Israel that God will rescue from mighty Babylon to bring home for a new beginning. This seedling becomes a majestic cedar in which all winged creatures find refuge. This is a figure for the eschatological ingathering of all the Gentile nations under the umbrella of Israel. The final verses articulate the reversal that will be brought about by God's hand. As proposed above, the juxtaposition of this reading with the parable of the mustard seed highlights the paradox in the latter of the two contrasting images of power. Alternatively, when linked with the parable of the growing seed, it can offer assurance of future flourishing of what appears insignificant and powerless in the present.

The responsorial psalm (92:2-3, 13-14, 15-16), also brings forward the image of a flourishing Lebanon cedar (vv. 13-14), but here the image has a different meaning. In the Psalm it is the just one who flourishes like a palm tree and grows like a cedar; they that are planted in God's courts are those who bear fruit. Here individuals who act uprightly prosper. In the reading from Ezekiel the tree represents Israel collectively and in the Gospel parables the growing plants are images for the reign of God, rather than faithful individuals.

In the second reading from 2 Corinthians 5:6-10, a loose connection can be seen between Paul's phrase "we walk by faith, not by sight" and the sower in the parable of the growing seed who knows not how the seed sprouts and grows.

EXCURSUS: THE KINGDOM OF GOD

The parables of the growing seed and the mustard plant are the first two parables that are explicitly about the "kingdom of God" (4:26, 30). The phrase *basileia tou theou*, "kingdom of God," appears fourteen times in the Gospel of Mark.[25] It is difficult to find an adequate phrase in English to convey the meaning of *basileia tou theou*. Translating it as "kingdom of God" is problematic, first, because it conveys the notion of a locale with fixed boundaries. It has long been recognized that God's *basileia* signifies divine "kingly rule" or "reign," not "kingdom" in a territorial sense.

A further difficulty with the translation "kingdom of God" is that it presents an image of God as king, reinforcing a male, monarchical model of God's rule. For communities of believers whose experience of governance is democratic, and who have become conscious of the limitations and dangers of having solely male images of God, "kingdom" is an inadequate term.[26]

Finally, in a first-century Palestinian context the term *basileia* would first call to mind the Roman imperial system of domination and exploitation. Jesus' annunciation of the *basileia* of God offered an alternative vision to that of the empire of Rome. The *basileia* that Jesus announced was one in which there was no more victimization or domination. This *basileia* was already present incipiently in Jesus' healing and liberative practices, the inclusive table sharing of his followers, and their domination-free relationships. The political threat that such a subversive *basileia* vision presented to the Roman imperial system is clear from the crucifixion of Jesus.[27]

Recognizing that no phrase adequately captures all that *basileia tou theou* signifies, alternative translations of *basileia* include: "kin-dom," "rule," "reign," "realm," "empire," "domain," and "commonweal." With adequate explanation, some leave it untranslated, as *basileia*. While none of these terms is perfect, it is helpful for a preacher to experiment with new phrases to jog the hearers into wrestling with the meaning of the phrase.

---

[25] Mark 1:15; 4:11, 26, 30; 9:1, 47; 10:14, 15, 23, 24, 25; 12:34; 14:25; 15:43.

[26] See Sallie McFague, *Models of God. Theology for an Ecological, Nuclear Age* (Philadelphia: Fortress, 1987).

[27] Elisabeth Schüssler Fiorenza, *Jesus: Miriam's Child, Sophia's Prophet* (New York: Continuum, 1994) 92–93.

It is important that whatever translation one adopts, it convey the sense of God's saving power over all creation, already inaugurated in a new way with the incarnation and ministry of Jesus. It is continued in the faithful ministry of the believing community, but not yet fully manifest. It is not a fixed place located in the beyond. Nor is it coterminus with the Church. It is authoritative power and empowerment by God-with-us.

CHAPTER SEVEN

Defilement from Within
(Mark 7:1-8, 14-15, 21-23)

Twenty-Second Sunday of Ordinary Time

*When the Pharisees with some scribes who had come from Jerusalem
    gathered around Jesus,
    they observed that some of his disciples ate their meals
    with unclean, that is, unwashed, hands.*
*—For the Pharisees and, in fact, all Jews,
    do not eat without carefully washing their hands,
    keeping the tradition of the elders.*
*And on coming from the marketplace
    they do not eat without purifying themselves.*
*And there are many other things that they have traditionally
        observed,
    the purification of cups and jugs and kettles and beds.—*
*So the Pharisees and scribes questioned him,
    "Why do your disciples not follow the tradition of the elders
    but instead eat a meal with unclean hands?"*
*He responded,
    "Well did Isaiah prophesy about you hypocrites, as it is
        written:*

This people honors me with their lips,
    but their hearts are far from me;
in vain do they worship me,
    teaching as doctrines human precepts.
*You disregard God's commandment but cling to human
        tradition."*
*He summoned the crowd again and said to them,
    "Hear me, all of you, and understand.*
*Nothing that enters one from outside can defile that person;
    but the things that come out from within are what defile.*

"From within people, from their hearts,
  come evil thoughts, unchastity, theft, murder,
  adultery, greed, malice, deceit,
  licentiousness, envy, blasphemy, arrogance, folly.
  All these evils come from within and they defile."

MARCAN LITERARY CONTEXT

Because some verses from Mark 7:1-23 are skipped in the lectionary selection, it is not immediately apparent that there is a parable in this passage.[1] Mark 7:17 clearly labels v. 15 a parable: "When he got home away from the crowd his disciples questioned him about the parable." The structure is reminiscent of 4:10-12, where the disciples ask Jesus for a private explanation of the parable of the sower/seed/harvest/soil. As in 4:13-20, so too in 7:18-23 Jesus interprets the enigmatic parable for his followers. Only the last three verses of the explanation appear in the lectionary. The summons to hear and understand in 7:14 also echoes 4:3, 9, 12, 23.[2]

The parable in v. 15 is preceded by the Pharisees and scribes questioning Jesus about his disciples eating with unclean hands. This section also echoes a previous scene, Mark 3:18-22, where Jesus is questioned about his disciples' practice of not fasting. The whole section can be outlined thus:[3]

A. Introduction and question (vv. 1-5)
   1. Pharisees and scribes criticize the negligence of the
       disciples
       (vv. 1-2; explanatory note in vv. 3-4)
   2. Question concerning
       a. tradition (in general, v. 5b)
       b. unwashed hands (particular case, v. 5c)

---

[1] For the ancients, παραβολή, "parable," or מָשָׁל, "mashal," could be used of any speech that was out of the ordinary or in some way striking or obscure. See further Madeleine Boucher, *The Mysterious Parable* (CBQMS 6; Washington, D.C.: CBA, 1977) 66.

[2] The connection to chap. 4 was also apparent to early scribes who added at v. 16, "Anyone who has ears to hear ought to hear," echoing 4:9, 23. Verse 16 is lacking in some of the best Greek manuscripts and is probably a later scribal addition.

[3] Lambrecht, *Once More Astonished*, 123.

B. Jesus' answer (vv. 6-23)
   1. Tradition (not a real answer as such to the Pharisees and scribes)
      a. vv. 6-8: counter-accusation (Isaiah quotation)
      b. vv. 9-13: concrete example (Corban case)
   2. Defilement
      a. vv. 14-15: answer to the people
         v. 15a: what does not defile
         v. 15b: what does defile
      b. vv. 17-23: explanation to the disciples of foregoing answer
         vv. 18c-19: what does not defile
         vv. 20-23: what does defile

This whole discourse likely underwent a long process of development before it reached its present form. It is possible that the parable in v. 15 is the oldest piece of tradition to which were added the narrative of an incident leading up to it and catechetical explanatory expansions following it.[4]

The introductory challenge by the Pharisees and scribes brings back on stage opponents of Jesus that have appeared earlier in the Gospel and who will continue to dispute with him. This is the first instance in which the two appear together as adversaries of Jesus. From a narrative perspective, the detail that they have come from Jerusalem (see also 3:22) implies that word about Jesus has spread even to the seat of Judaism and has provoked opposition there.[5]

---

[4] Lambrecht, *Once More Astonished*, 123; Eduard Schweizer, *The Good News According to Mark* (Richmond: John Knox, 1970) 146. For a detailed redaction-critical analysis see Elian Cuvillier, *Le concept de PARABOLH dans le second évangile* (EB n.s. 19; Paris: Gabalda, 1993) 153–70.

[5] Whether there were Pharisees in Galilee in the time of Jesus is a matter of debate. Seán Freyne (*Galilee from Alexander the Great to Hadrian 323 B.C.E. to 135 C.E.* [University of Notre Dame Center for the Study of Judaism and Christianity in Antiquity 5; Wilmington, Del. and Notre Dame, Ind.: Glazier and University of Notre Dame Press, 1980] 305–43) argues for the presence of some Pharisees in Galilee. Other scholars, e.g., Jacob Neusner (*From Politics to Piety. The Emergence of Pharisaic Judaism* [Englewood Cliffs, N.J.: Prentice Hall, 1973] 72) interpret such references to Pharisees and scribes in the Gospels as a narrative convention for opponents to Jesus.

PURITY PRACTICES (vv. 1-8)

The controversy concerns some of Jesus' disciples who eat with unwashed hands (v. 2). Verses 3 and 4 are an aside to Mark's Gentile audience, explaining Jewish purity customs. These customs are not a matter of hygiene, but concern the social systems by which boundaries of belonging are defined. Purity and cleanness have to do with what is in its proper place; impurity and uncleanness deals with what is out of place. Purity distinctions are drawn for times, places, persons, things, meals, and "others" (who can pollute by contact).[6]

The custom of ritual washing has its roots in the mandate in Exodus 30:19; 40:12 that priests wash their hands and feet before entering into the tent of meeting. By the second century B.C.E. a number of Jews had voluntarily assumed the priestly practices of washing their hands[7] before morning prayer and before eating. Some wanted to impose these and other such observances on all Jews.[8] For Pharisees this oral interpretation of the Law was as binding as the written Law.[9]

This "tradition of the elders" (v. 3), was largely defined, maintained, and observed by urban elites. Full observance was nearly impossible for peasant farmers, fishermen, and itinerants such as Jesus, due to scarcity of water for ritual ablutions and contact with dead fish and other pollutants.[10]

Jesus' response to the challenge of the Jewish leaders is not a direct answer to their question. His reply comes in two parts. In vv. 6-8 he calls upon Scripture to pose a counter-challenge, which is illustrated by a particular case in vv. 9-13. This second part is omitted from the lectionary reading. In v. 6 Jesus labels his opponents as hypocrites. The Greek term *hypokritēs*, "hypocrite," denotes a stage actor. Its appearance on

---

[6] Malina and Rohrbaugh, *Social Science Commentary*, 222–24; Jerome Neyrey, "The Idea of Purity in Mark's Gospel," *Semeia* 35 (1986) 91–128.

[7] In Mark 7:4 the washing extends also the utensils for preparing meals; *klinē*, "bed," most likely refers to a dining couch.

[8] Stock, *Mark*, 201.

[9] The oral interpretations of the rabbis were fixed in written form in the Mishnah and Talmud beginning in the second century C.E.

[10] Malina and Rohrbaugh, *Social Science Commentary*, 221; Pilch, *Cultural World*, 130.

the lips of Jesus in all three Synoptic gospels[11] may indicate Jesus' familiarity with the theatre. Such is possible from his contact with the large Hellenistic city of Sepphoris, only four miles from his hometown of Nazareth.[12]

Jesus accuses his opponents of putting on an identity not their own and performing for the approval of others. Just as Isaiah (29:13)[13] charged, these people pay lip-service to God while their hearts are elsewhere. Moreover they substitute observance of their humanly contrived practices for what the Law of Moses commanded (v. 7). From a social-science perspective, Jesus gains honor in this exchange by his ability to draw creatively upon the tradition in the heat of conflict.[14] That his challengers make no come-back implies that he wins the argument.

WHAT COMES OUT (vv. 14-23)

In the second half of the passage Jesus addresses first the crowd (vv. 14-15) and then his disciples (vv. 17-23). While there are links with 7:1-13, there is a shift in focus from a manner of eating that may or may not be polluting to what foods are defiling. The parable (v. 15), however, concerns far more than food. While v. 19 (which is omitted from the lectionary) interprets Jesus' saying as "Thus he declared all foods clean," vv. 21-23 widen the topic beyond food.[15] Verses 18-20 explain, "everything that goes into a person from outside cannot defile, since it enters not the heart but the stomach and passes out into

---

[11] Only here in Mark; thirteen times in Matthew and three times in Luke.

[12] See Richard A. Batey, "Jesus and the Theatre," *NTS* 30 (1984) 564-65; Agustine Stock, "Jesus, Hypocrites, and Herodians, *BTB* 16 (1986) 3–7.

[13] The quotation of Isaiah 29:13 in vv. 6-7 follows the wording of the Septuagint (the Greek translation of the Hebrew Scriptures). The final phrase, "teaching as doctrines human precepts" is not found in the Hebrew version.

[14] Pilch, *Cultural World*, 131.

[15] The end of v. 19, "Thus he declared all foods clean," is clearly an interpretation added later. Purity practices regarding food constituted one of the biggest stumbling blocks between Jewish and Gentile Christians in the early church (e.g., Acts 10:1–11:18; 15:1-29; Gal 2:1-9). Had the earthly Jesus resolved the question during his ministry as Mark 7:19 asserts, these conflicts would not have arisen.

the latrine . . . But what comes out of a person, that is what defiles." Verse 21, where the lectionary selection resumes, picks up on the theme of what is in the heart, echoing 7:19 and the Isaiah quotation in Mark 7:6. What goes into the stomach is of no import; what comes from the heart is what matters.

In this section Jesus' further elaboration on the "heart" continues developing the metaphor presented in the Isaiah quote (7:6) directed to the Pharisees and scribes. Now Jesus directs his remarks as a warning to his disciples, implicitly prolonging the contrast between their behavior and that of the Pharisees and scribes. "Heart" is used very often in both Testaments in a figurative sense as the source of all emotions, passions, and intellectual life. It is the seat of one's will and the center of one's relationship with God. It is the heart that speaks to God (Ps 27:8) and receives God's word (Deut 30:14). God gives hearts understanding (1 Kgs 3:9) and inspires hearts to action (Neh 2:12).[16] What proceeds from the heart (Mark 7:21), then, is indicative of one's relationship with God.

The list of vices in vv. 21-22 is similar to those found also in Rom 1:29-31 and Gal 5:19-21. Such lists were also used by Hellenistic philosophers and served as catechetical devices. Three of the vices in Mark 7, theft, murder, and adultery, appear in Hosea's accusations against Israel (Hos 4:2) and are also forbidden in the Decalogue (Exod 20:13-17; Deut 5:17-22). Two of the evils named are elsewhere attributed by Mark to Jesus' opponents.[17] Murder is the crime imputed to Barabbas (15:7) and deceit is the means by which the high priests and scribes intend to arrest Jesus (14:1).

PREACHING POSSIBILITIES

The first part of the reading provides an opportunity for disciples to reflect on motivation for external practices. If, as Jesus accused the Pharisees and scribes, a liturgical practice or a religious custom that was good in its origin has deteriorated

---

[16] For extensive biblical references to the "heart" see Thomas P. McCreesh, "Heart," *The Collegeville Pastoral Dictionary of Biblical Theology* (Collegeville: The Liturgical Press, 1996) 422–24.

[17] Myers, *Binding the Strong Man*, 220.

into a showy external observance, then one must move toward action that will allow encounter with God that moves the heart. A preacher must be wary not to present Jesus in today's Gospel as denouncing all of the Law or declaring the whole of Jewish practice obsolete. Rather, like a prophet from of old, he challenges those whose fulfillment of the Law is external or merely ceremonial (e.g., Isa 1:11-17; Jer 7:21-26; Amos 5:21-27). Like the prophets, Jesus does not eliminate cultic practices, but insists that they be accompanied by acts of justice toward one's neighbor that flow from right relation with God.[18] Jesus, in accord with the Law, continues to denounce the same evils that are proscribed in the Ten Commandments. Theft, murder, adultery, deceit, and envy (vv. 21-22) explicitly recall the Decalogue.

While the accusation of hypocrisy in the first part of the passage might suggest a theme of contrasting external deeds with one's internal life, the second half clearly connects the two, rather than placing them in opposition. From within people, from their hearts, flow actions that reflect their interior life with God, or the lack thereof. The interior life and its external manifestation must be in harmony.

LECTIONARY CONTEXT

On this particular Sunday there is a close thematic connection among all the readings. The first reading from Deuteronomy (4:1-2, 6-8) comes just before Moses' giving of the Ten Commandments to Israel. It is an exhortation to hear and observe carefully all the statutes and decrees of God, neither adding to nor taking away anything from them. Israel's reward will be possession of the land and a reputation before other nations for wisdom and closeness to God.

The responsorial psalm (15:2-3, 3-4, 4-5) was composed for use at the Temple gate to declare who was worthy for entrance. Like the Gospel, it links what a person thinks in the heart (v. 2) with their actions toward others. Only one who acts justly toward others can enter into the presence of God for

---

[18] Madeline Boucher, *The Mysterious Parable*, CBQMS 6 (Washington, D.C.: Catholic Biblical Association of America, 1977) 67.

worship. In turn, encounter with God leads to further right relation with people.

The second reading from James (1:17-18, 21b-22, 27) echoes
the same theme: one who does not act on the word that is received is deluded. While the responsorial psalm and the Gospel
list specific actions and vices to be avoided, the reading from
James defines religion that is pure and undefiled before God
as "care for orphans and widows." It is one's treatment of the
poorest and most disadvantaged that reveals one's true relationship with God.

CHAPTER EIGHT

Figs and Future

(Mark 13:24-32)

Thirty-Third Sunday in Ordinary Time

Jesus said to his disciples:
"In those days after that tribulation
the sun will be darkened,
and the moon will not give its light,
and the stars will be falling from the sky,
and the powers in the heavens will be shaken.

"And then they will see 'the Son of Man coming in the clouds'
with great power and glory,
and then he will send out the angels
and gather his elect from the four winds,
from the end of the earth to the end of the sky.

"Learn a lesson from the fig tree.
When its branch becomes tender and sprouts leaves,
you know that summer is near.
In the same way, when you see these things happening,
know that he is near, at the gates.
Amen, I say to you,
this generation will not pass away
until all these things have taken place.
Heaven and earth will pass away,
but my words will not pass away.

"But of that day or hour, no one knows,
neither the angels in heaven, nor the Son, but only the Father."

MARCAN LITERARY CONTEXT

This passage comes toward the end of Mark 13, a long discourse addressed by Jesus to an inner circle of disciples, Peter, James, John, and Andrew (13:3). They are sitting on the

Mount of Olives facing the Temple (13:3) and the disciples ask Jesus about signs pointing to the end. In some ways Mark 13 functions similarly to John 14–17 and Luke 22, as a farewell discourse by Jesus.[1] But the predominant feature in Mark 13 is its apocalyptic genre. As such, it is not a literal prediction of future events, but is a form of literary prophecy that had wide popularity in both Jewish and Christian circles from 200 B.C.E. to 200 C.E. It arose as a means to provide hope to believers who experienced erosion of values from within their faith communities and attack from outsiders. In such a time of crisis, apocalyptic writing attempts to maintain the faith and hope of believers by revealing (the Greek word *apokalypsis*, "apocalypse," means "revelation") the end of history, soon to come, in which God would intervene and reverse the present status.[2] Those presently persecuted unjustly would be rewarded, while evil ones would receive punishment.

The structure of Mark 13 can be shown to be concentric:[3]

Introduction (vv. 1-4)

Discourse (vv. 5-37):

A Oppression: information and warning (vv. 5b-23)
   a deceivers (vv. 5b-6): "Take heed . . ."
     b wars (vv. 7-8): "When you hear . . ."
       c persecutions (vv. 9-13): ". . . take heed . . ."
     b' war (vv. 14-20): ". . . when you see . . ."
   a' deceivers (vv. 21-23): ". . . take heed . . ."
B Coming: announcement (vv. 24-27)
A' The Day and the Hour: information and warning (vv. 28-36)
   a parable of the Budding Fig Tree (vv. 28-29)
   b logion about the certain and imminent return (v. 30)

---

[1] See also Moses' farewell in Deuteronomy 32. This was a common literary genre in which a great man gathers his disciples on the eve of his death and gives them instructions for the future. See Raymond Brown, *The Gospel According to John XIII-XXI* (AB29A; Garden City, N.J.: Doubleday, 1970) 598.

[2] See Adela Yarbro Collins, "The Apocalyptic Rhetoric of Mark 13 in Historical Context," *BR* 41 (1996) 5–36, who proposes that Mark 13 responds to the historical situation after the summer of 66 C.E., when Menachem emerged as a messianic leader, and before the destruction of the Temple in 70 C.E.

[3] Lambrecht, *Once More Astonished*, 133; similarly van Iersel, *Mark*, 159–60.

    c confirmation logion (v. 31)
    b' logion about the sudden, unexpected return (v. 32)
   A' parable of the Doorkeeper (vv. 33-36)
Concluding verse (v. 37)

In this outline, chapter 13 has three major sections. The first (vv. 5b-23) warns against deceivers and announces the coming persecution. It also issues reassurance of assistance from the holy Spirit and exhorts the hearers to persevere. The third section (vv. 28-36) focuses on the timing of the end and urges watchfulness. These sections frame the central part (vv. 24-27) that announces the coming of the Human One and his gathering of the elect.

The tribulations announced in this chapter reflect the actual situation of the Marcan community. With this discourse the evangelist attempts to dispel both an over-anxious expectation by some people of an immediate end as well as an exaggerated apocalyptic mentality of others who interpreted particular events as signs that the end had already come.

The portion selected for the lectionary for this Sunday begins with the central section, the announcement of the coming of the Human One, followed by the first of the two parables concerning the timing. The use of this reading at the close of the liturgical year serves to heighten the sense of end-timing.

THE COMING OF THE HUMAN ONE (13:24-27)

The opening phrase, "In those days after that tribulation," refers back to v. 17 that describes woes to pregnant women and nursing mothers "in those days" and to v. 19 that declares, "for those times will have tribulation such as has not been since the beginning of God's creation until now." The mention of creation in v. 19 prepares for the imagery in v. 24, where the darkening of the sun, moon, and stars symbolizes an undoing of creation (Gen 1:14-18) and a preparation for a new period of creation at the parousia.[4]

Next the coming of the Human One is described (v. 26). The phrase "Son of Man" occurs fourteen times in the Gospel

---

[4] Stock, *Mark*, 339.

of Mark. It is always placed on the lips of Jesus and is used in three contexts: to speak of Jesus' earthly activity, his passion, and his eschatological function.[5] There is some debate among scholars as to the origin and meaning of the phrase. Some think its background comes from uses of the phrase in Daniel 7:13 and *1 Enoch* 37–71 where it refers to an apocalyptic figure carrying out God's salvation and judgment. Others advance that the phrase was simply a circumlocution for a human person, similar to the phrase בֶּן־אָדָם (*ben ʾadam*, "son of man") in Psalm 8:6 [4], with the sense of "someone," or "I." For some scholars the phrase does not date to Jesus, but was introduced by the early Christian community. One thing all agree on is that by the time the Gospels are composed the phrase has taken on the function of a christological title.[6]

The description of the end-time coming of the Son, "'in the clouds' with great power and glory" is repeated in Mark 14:62, where Jesus breaks his silence before the high priest, confirming that he is the Messiah. The Son's sending out of his angels to gather in the elect (v. 27) issues a word of comfort to those who wait with patient endurance. There is no mention of judgment; the whole emphasis here is on the promise of hope for those who remain faithful.

FLOWERING FIGS

After this reassuring portrayal of the end time follows a parable about its nearness. In the introductory verse the word *parabolē* ("parable") has a slightly different nuance than elsewhere. Here it is usually translated "lesson." The "parable" of the fig tree, rather than convey a puzzle in enigmatic speech, functions as an illustration to clarify the sayings about the end. The point is readily apparent.[7] The fig tree, different from other

---

[5] Of Jesus' earthly activity: Mark 2:10, 28; of his passion: Mark 8:31; 9:9, 12, 31; 10:33, 45; 14:21 (2x), 41; of his glorious coming: Mark 8:38; 13:26; 14:62.

[6] For detailed philological analysis see Joseph A. Fitzmyer, "The New Testament Title 'Son of Man' Philologically Considered," in *A Wandering Aramean. Collected Aramaic Essays* (SBLMS 25; Chico, Calif.: Scholars Press, 1979) 143–60.

[7] In contrast to Mark 4, where the parables are addressed to the crowds and then explained privately to the disciples, Mark 13 begins with Jesus speak-

trees in Palestine,[8] sheds all its leaves in winter. Its budding is a sign of the coming of summer.[9] Just so, the signs of the end, described in the earlier verses[10] of Mark 13 that are not part of this reading, point toward the nearness of the Human One.

For those who are hearing or reading the Gospel as a continuous narrative, the mention of a fig tree recalls the episode in Mark 11:12-14, 20-25. On the day after Jesus entered Jerusalem he cursed the fruitless fig (vv. 12-14), which the disciples found withered to its roots on the morrow (vv. 20-25). The two parts of the incident frame Jesus' casting out of the money changers from the Temple (11:15-29). In this context the unproductive fig symbolizes the Temple leadership whose demise Jesus enacts symbolically. The use of a fig tree in 13:28-29 changes its symbolism to one of promise of new life. Mark deftly employs two sides of the fig tree's eschatological symbolism. With the coming of Jesus to Jerusalem the fig withers under his judgment. With the end-time coming of the Human One, the fig once again blooms with new life and blessing.[11]

The parable cuts two ways: for those who are discouraged about the delay in the coming of the parousia it gives encouragement about its nearness. For those who interpret present disasters, wars, and persecution as signs that the end has already come, it corrects their mistaken notion and exhorts them to continue steadfast into the future.

---

ing privately to his disciples (v. 3) and ends with an exhortation, "What I say to you, I say to all" (13:37). The parables of the fig tree and the doorkeeper are plain illustrations and do not require private interpretation from Jesus.

  [8] Most trees in Palestine are evergreens.

  [9] There are only two seasons in Palestine: summer, which is dry and hot, and winter, or the rainy season. There is a brief interchange period between the two, but no autumn or spring per se.

  [10] The word *tauta*, "these things," in v. 29 refers to all the signs described in chapter 13, forming an inclusio with v. 4, where the disciples had asked Jesus to tell them "when will these things *(tauta)* happen."

  [11] In biblical tradition the fig tree often functions as a metaphor for both blessings and curses, e.g., Deuteronomy 8:7-8; 1 Kings 4:25; Hosea 9:10; Micah 4:4; Amos 4:9; Jeremiah 24:2; Joel 1:6-7. See Bernard Brandon Scott, *Hear Then the Parable* (Minneapolis: Fortress, 1989) 332–34; William Telford, *The Barren Temple and the Withered Tree* (JSNTSup 1; Sheffield: JSOT, 1980) 213–18.

There is some tension between v. 30 and v. 32 about the timing of the end. Verse 30 implies certitude that the end can be expected imminently: before the death of the present generation (so also Mark 9:1). Verse 32 seems to contradict this with the assertion that no one but the Father knows the timing. The two can be seen to function in tandem, as do the two parables of the fig tree (vv. 28-29) and the doorkeeper (vv. 34-35): they stress different aspects of the question of timing. The first gives reassurance to those becoming weary; the second accents the need for watchfulness since the exact time is unknown.

The verse that stands at the center of these sayings (v. 31) asserts the absolute reliability of Jesus' message. It is solemnly introduced with an oath formula, "Amen, I say to you." The function of an oath is to show that the one pronouncing it is honorable and to make clear what may appear ambiguous or incredible about that person's claims. The oath in v. 31 rests on the understanding that from an Israelite point of view, God's creation is good and belongs to God and will last forever. The force of Jesus' saying is that it is just as impossible for his words to pass away as it is for God's creation to pass away.[12]

PREACHING POSSIBILITIES

While Mark's community lived in imminent expectation of the end times, as did many early Christians (e.g., Paul in 1 Thess 4:15), most believers today do not anticipate the parousia in their lifetime, much less give it all that much thought. After almost two thousand years the edge of expectation has diminished and all but select groups of apocalyptically-oriented Christians have settled into day-to-day efforts at long-term Christian living. Nonetheless, this Gospel passage can still offer hope in the face of persecution, struggles, and discouragement in the between-times.

One should resist trying to interpret literally the happenings described in Mark 13 as signs of the end times. Cataclysmic events of every age have been thus interpreted. Rather, it is important to recognize that Mark is using stock apocalyptic symbols. Cosmic portents of judgment are common in apocalyptic

---

[12] Malina and Rohrbaugh, *Social Science Commentary*, 263.

and late prophetic literature.[13] The notion of "falling" or being cast out from heaven is found in Luke 10:18; John 12:31; Rev 12:9. The "gathering up" of the elect from the four corners has echoes in 1 Thessalonians 4:16-17; Deuteronomy 30:4. A cloud frequently serves as a vehicle of transport in apocalyptic literature (Dan 7:13; 1 Thess 4:17; Rev 1:7; 11:12; 14:14) and angels are standard apocalyptic divine messengers or guides.

A more fruitful reflection on such texts is to understand how apocalyptic writing functioned and to relate it to contemporary situations. This genre aimed to give hope to people who were under duress, whether from internal strife or external threats. It can function the same way today. One way in which such texts can be preached is to counter passivity or hopelessness in the face of suffering. The Gospel emphasizes that although one cannot know the precise timing, there is an end to the present distress. God's ultimate victory in Christ gives hope that suffering and even death itself have been overcome. The fig tree symbol conveys the message that even out of utter destruction (11:12-14, 20-25) and appearance of death (as a leafless fig in winter) new life can blossom forth (13:28-29). Even wars, natural disasters, and famines can be labor pains (13:8) that precede new creation.

Finally, one caution about apocalyptic genre. The preacher should be aware of and denounce the kind of apocalyptic thinking that is based on a dualistic mentality that divides people into "us" and "them," as forces of absolute good against absolute evil. While such a construction of reality is understandable as a way to cope with persecution, it is very dangerous to think that through some combination of right belief and behavior one can be aligned absolutely with the good. Such thinking underlies sectarian divisions drawn by racial, ethnic, and religious lines and fuels campaigns of mass destruction of the "enemy." Apocalypticists applaud violence directed against "enemies" as evidence of God's punishment, while violence against themselves is interpreted as persecution of the righteous. They see both as signs of the end-times that anticipate

---

[13] E.g., *1 Enoch* 80:4-7; 4 Ezra 5:4; Isaiah 13:10; Ezekiel 32:7-8; Amos 8:9; Joel 2:10.

their own near deliverance. From such a stance the wellsprings of compassion are shut off toward those with whom one does not identify. Such believers may even oppose efforts to relieve poverty or prevent war, thinking that such will delay God's final intervention.[14]

LECTIONARY CONTEXT

The first reading from Daniel (12:1-3) is also cast in apocalyptic genre. It is one of the first clear references in the Hebrew Scriptures to belief in the resurrection. The brutal persecution in the time of Antiochus IV Epiphanes (175–164 B.C.E.) helped give rise to the belief that the righteous would enjoy an eternal reward in life after death.

The responsorial psalm (16:5, 8, 9-10, 11) expresses confidence in God's promises in a time of sickness or moral collapse. Despite present trials, God holds one fast. In the middle stanza there is a hint at belief in immortality, picking up a theme from the first reading. The psalm selection concludes on a note of joy, expressing utter confidence in dwelling in God's presence forever.

The second reading from Hebrews (10:11-14, 18) contrasts the sacrifice of Christ with the daily sacrifices of the Israelite priests that cannot take away sins. Christ's one offering has effected forgiveness, which makes the believer's destiny secure. In the context of the other readings it gives encouragement about the believer's ultimate fate.

---

[14] Rosemary Radford Ruether, *Gaia and God* (HarperSanFrancisco, 1992) 81–84.

CHAPTER NINE

Sower, Seed, Soil, and Harvest
(Mark 4:1-20)*

Wednesday of the Third Week of Ordinary Time

On another occasion [Jesus] began to teach by the sea.
A very large crowd gathered around him
   so that he got into a boat on the sea and sat down.
And the whole crowd was beside the sea on land.
And he taught them at length in parables,
   and in the course of his instruction he said to them,
   "Hear this! A sower went out to sow.
And as he sowed, some seed fell on the path,
   and the birds came and ate it up.
Other seed fell on rocky ground where it had little soil.
It sprang up at once because the soil was not deep.
And when the sun rose, it was scorched and it withered for lack of roots.
Some seed fell among thorns, and the thorns grew up and choked it
   and it produced no grain.
And some seed fell on rich soil and produced fruit.
It came up and grew and yielded thirty, sixty, and a hundredfold."
[Jesus] added, "Whoever has ears to hear ought to hear."

And when he was alone,
   those present along with the Twelve
   questioned him about the parables.
He answered them,
   "The mystery of the kingdom of God has been granted to you.
But to those outside everything comes in parables, so that

   'they may look and see but not perceive,
     and hear and listen but not understand,
   in order that they may not be converted and be forgiven.'"

   * At the time this book went to press, volume II of the revised *Lectionary for Mass* had not yet been approved by the Holy See. The texts given here are taken from the 1986 NAB translation of the New Testament which will be used in the *Lectionary*.

Jesus said to them, "Do you not understand this parable?
Then how will you understand any of the parables?
The sower sows the word.
These are the ones on the path where the word is sown.
As soon as they hear, Satan comes at once
and takes away the word sown in them.
And these are the ones sown on rocky ground who,
when they hear the word, receive it at once with joy.
But they have no root; they last only for a time.
Then when tribulation or persecution comes because of the word,
they quickly fall away.
Those sown among thorns are another sort.
They are the people who hear the word,
but worldly anxiety, the lure of riches,
and the craving for other things intrude and choke the word,
and it bears no fruit.
But those sown on rich soil are the ones who hear the word and accept it
and bear fruit thirty and sixty and a hundredfold."

MARCAN LITERARY CONTEXT

This Gospel selection has three parts: the parable proper
(4:1-9), a query to Jesus by the disciples about how to understand parables and his response (vv. 10-12), and an interpretation of the parable (vv. 13-20). This is the beginning of the
major collection of Marcan parables.[1] Only the Matthean version of this parable appears in the Sunday lectionary.

In the first three chapters of Mark's Gospel Jesus' ministry
centers on healing and exorcising. In chapter 4 the focus shifts
to his role as teacher. As with Jesus' powerful deeds, his words
will also provoke a divided response. Some will choose to follow him; others will turn away.

The opening verses (vv. 1-2) introduce a setting by the sea.
Throughout the first half of the Gospel of Mark the sea is the
geographical focal point.[2] Jesus calls the first disciples by the
sea (Mark 1:16, 19, 20; 2:13) and heals there (3:7-12). He exer-

---

[1] See above, chapter 6 for the structure of the whole of Mark 4. For more
detailed analysis of Marcan redactional intent see C. M. Tuckett, "Mark's Concerns in the Parables Chapter (Mark 4,1-34)" *Bib* 69 (1988) 1–26.
[2] See Elizabeth Struthers Malbon, "The Jesus of Mark and the Sea of
Galilee," *JBL* 103 (1984) 363–77.

cises mastery over the sea (4:35-41; 6:45-52), a power which is attributed to God in Psalm 107:23-32. He now teaches by the sea (4:1 so also 2:13). The audience for the first parables is a very large crowd gathered around Jesus (4:1). Jesus gets into a boat while the crowd stays on land for his instruction. One can envision a kind of natural amphitheater created by the sloping hills alongside the Sea of Galilee.[3] Jesus' seated position in the boat is not only practical but is also the standard position of a Jewish teacher.[4]

The parable proper (vv. 3-9) is framed with the exhortations, "Hear this!" (v. 3) and "Whoever has ears to hear ought to hear!" (v. 9). The admonition to "hear" recalls the *Shema*ᶜ, the prayer from Deuteronomy 6:4-5, prayed by observant Jews three times daily, "Hear, O Israel! The LORD is our God, the LORD alone! Therefore, you shall love the LORD, your God, with all your heart, and with all your soul, and with all your strength."[5] While this prayer underscores Israel's unique relationship with God, Jesus' parable widens the audience to any who will attend to his words.

But what is the meaning of his words? The parable allows for a variety of interpretations, depending on which "character" is chosen as the focus. It can be: The Parable of the Sower,[6] The Parable of the Seed,[7] The Parable of the Soil, and The Parable of the Harvest.[8]

---

[3] See Marianne Race and Laurie Brink, *In This Place. Reflections on the Land of the Gospels for the Liturgical Cycles* (Collegeville: The Liturgical Press, 1998) 103–04.

[4] See also Mark 9:35, where Jesus sits to instruct the disciples about his coming passion.

[5] Birger Gerhardsson, "The Parable of the Sower and Its Interpretation," *NTS* 14 (1968) 165–93 interprets the whole parable in light of the Deuteronomic referent. For him the seed devoured by birds represents those who do not love God with their whole heart; those on rocky ground are those who do not love God with their souls; those choked by thorns are those who fail to love God with their whole might.

[6] So *NAB, NJB, La Nueva Biblia Latinoamericana, Christian Community Bible*.

[7] So 1970 edition of the NAB.

[8] The *NRSV* wisely avoids titling the parable, allowing for any of the various interpretations. The *Revised English Bible* titles the whole of chapter 4, "Parables." No parable is entitled in the Greek text.

THE PARABLE OF THE SOWER

The opening line of the parable draws attention to the sower, a familiar character in rural Palestine. If Jesus' original audience were peasant farmers, who saw the sower as their landowner, they might react with disdain toward the sloppy and wasteful manner of sowing.[9] Alternatively, if they saw the sower as a tenant farmer or a day laborer like themselves, their reaction would be sympathetic. They would know all too well the amount of seed and effort that is expended that never bears fruit because of the difficult conditions.[10]

The sower is usually interpreted as representing God or Jesus, and the seed is the word of God (4:14). From this perspective the story centers on how God acts. God is like a profligate farmer, who indiscriminately sows seed on every type of ground. The story is an illustration of God's all-inclusive love. The point is that God knowingly scatters the seed on all types of soil. God offers the word to every person, regardless of their potential for accepting it. Although not all will accept the word and bring it to fruition, it is offered to all. If the sower is Jesus, the point is the same. Jesus preaches the word to all, offering God's inclusive love indiscriminately to all kinds of people.

In the first-century Palestinian world of Jesus this crossing of boundaries and mixing of peoples would be shocking.[11] If Jesus' peasant audience has regarded the sower with hostility, seeing in him the figure of a wasteful landlord, there is a challenge to them that God can be manifest even in the one they regard as despicable. If they were to exercise God's all-inclusive love, it must extend even to one who exploits them. Such inclusive love does not mean that exploitation goes unchallenged. Rather, it creates an opportunity for an oppressor to repent; it does not simply cut off such a one as unredeemable.

---

[9] There is some debate whether the custom was to plow after sowing, as this parable envisions. Some ancient texts refer to plowing before sowing: Isaiah 28:24-26; Jeremiah 4:3; Ezekiel 36:9; *Gos.Thom.* 20; Pliny, *Nat.Hist.* 18.176. Others speak of plowing after sowing: *Jub.* 11.11; *m. Šabb.* 7.2; *b. Šabb.* 73a-b.

[10] Malina and Rohrbaugh, *Social Science Commentary*, 202.

[11] Ibid., 192–94; David Rhoads, "Social Criticism: Crossing Boundaries," in *New Approaches in Biblical Studies*, ed. J. C. Anderson and S. D. Moore (Minneapolis: Fortress, 1992) 135-61.

Alternatively, if the peasants identify with the sower as one like themselves, the challenge is for them to understand that in their own actions they emulate God whenever their actions of sowing God's word extend beyond their own circles of friends and relations.

From the narrative perspective of the Gospel text, the invitation to the crowds who are not yet followers of Jesus is to receive and respond to the gracious word he preaches. If they are Jews who think they already know and are obedient to God, Jesus invites them to expand their perception of who it is God invites to be among the chosen ones. For people in the crowd who see themselves outside the bounds of Israel, or not addressed by Israel's God, a door is now opened to them.

From the standpoint of Mark's community the parable justifies the inclusion of marginal Jews and Gentile members among the faithful. The sower has scattered seed among those formerly not regarded as "good soil." For contemporary Christian communities that struggle with inclusivity, the parable can function the same way.

THE PARABLE OF THE SEED

If the seed is the focus of the parable, then the point shifts to the reliability of the seed to bring forth a yield. Though it appears at first that there will be no harvest, the end result confirms the seed's efficacy. The parable assures that God's word does accomplish its purpose, even though much of it falls on deaf ears.

The parable may well be a recasting of Isaiah 55:10-11: "For as the rain and the snow come down from heaven, / and do not return there until they have watered the earth, / making it bring forth and sprout, / giving seed to the sower and bread to the eater, so shall my word be that goes out from my mouth; / it shall not return to me empty, / but it shall accomplish that which I purpose, / and succeed in the thing for which I sent it" (NRSV).[12]

---

[12] C. A. Evans ("A Note on the Function of Isaiah 6:9-10 in Mark 4," *RB* 99 [1981] 234–35) analyzes the Marcan version of the parable as a midrash on Isa 6:9-13 and Isa 55:10-11. See also J. W. Bowker, "Mystery and Parable: Mark 4:1-20," *JTS* 25 (1974) 300–17, who sees Mark 4:1-20 as a midrash on Isaiah 6:13.

In the context of Jesus' ministry, the parable encourages his disciples that, despite the lack of an overwhelmingly positive response, Jesus' preaching of God's word does, finally, achieve God's purpose. Christians today can take the same assurance from the parable; despite lack of apparent initial results, their efforts at spreading God's word will eventually bring forth fruit.

THE PARABLE OF THE HARVEST

Another point emerges if the focus of the parable is the harvest. The narrative creates a dynamic in which expectations rise with each arena of sowing. From the footpath, hopes of harvest are immediately dashed as the birds instantly devour the seed. From the rocky ground, hope springs up immediately with the sprouting seed, but, again, is short-lived. From the thorn patch, hope endures a bit longer, as the seed and the thorns both grow up. But in the end the thorns triumph. Finally, from the good soil comes grain that reaches maturity.

But the story does more than build to an expected climax. It is not simply an assurance of eventual success in the face of repeated failure. The staggering amounts of the harvest shatter open the parable, and propel the hearer into an eschatological scenario. The image of harvest is often used to speak of the end time,[13] as is hyperbole.[14] The amounts of the harvest are astronomical. If a good harvest for a Palestinian farmer yields up to ten-fold, one that produces thirty, sixty, or one-hundred-fold is unimaginable.[15] This explosive scale symbolizes the overflowing of divine fullness, which surpasses all human measure.[16]

---

[13] So also Mark 4:29; Matthew 13:30, 39; 21:34, 41.

[14] Irenaeus (*Adv. Haer.* 5.33.3-4) asserts that Papias foretold that in messianic times "a grain of wheat shall bring forth 10,000 ears, and every ear shall have 10,000 grains." The rabbinic tractate *Ketub.* 111b–112a says it will take a ship to carry one grape in the messianic age.

[15] Jeremias (*Parables*, 150, n. 84) asserts that a good harvest yields up to ten-fold; an average one seven and a half.

[16] A similar point is found in Genesis 26:12, "Isaac sowed seed in that land, and in the same year reaped a hundredfold. The LORD blessed him."

Considered from this perspective, whether the context is Jesus' preaching, or Mark's community, or contemporary proclamation of the gospel, the parable leaves the hearer overwhelmed at the inconceivable abundance of God's graciousness manifest in the end times. It evokes awe and praise of God, as the miraculous harvest is clearly the work of God, surpassing anything that is possible from human efforts. A peasant farmer who has labored mightily against adverse conditions hears in this story good news of God's loving providence toward those in need and assurance of great reward in the end time.[17]

In light of Jesus' proclamation in Mark 1:14-15, that the reign of God is already at hand, some commentators read the abundant harvest as articulating the hopes of oppressed people for a present re-ordering of relationships.[18] It is not just wishful dreaming for the future, but has a subversive function in the present. The bumper crop could shatter the vassal relationship between peasant and landlord. With such a surplus a farmer who formerly struggled just to eat and pay his debts could think outrageous thoughts of even buying the land himself. His oppressive servitude to the landowner could come to an end.

UNDERSTANDING THE PARABLES (4:10-12)

Sandwiched between the parable (vv. 1-9) and its explanation (vv. 13-20) is a discussion about how to understand the parables. Jesus' response draws a clear line between insiders and outsiders. The former are given "the mysteries of the kingdom of God," but to those outside, everything is in parables. Using the words of the prophet Isaiah (6:9) Jesus seems to leave little hope for those who do not perceive or understand (v. 12).

---

[17] John J. Pilch (*The Cultural World of the Gospel. Sunday by Sunday Cycle A* [Collegeville: The Liturgical Press, 1996] 109) notes that if Jesus' audience heard the parable as telling of a wasteful owner who realized such an enormous profit, it would hardly be good news. We would wonder, then, why Jesus would tell such a story that depicts the way things are in an oppressive situation without offering any hopeful alternative.

[18] Ched Myers, *Binding the Strong Man,* 177.

Scholars have wrestled mightily with the meaning of these verses.[19] Are the parables meant to be unintelligible? Does Jesus intend to keep some people on the outside? If so, how can this be reconciled with his universal saving purpose? One explanation is that Jesus is following an established rabbinical parable pattern in which there are four parts: (1) a question posed by an opponent, (2) a public retort, in veiled language, sufficient to silence the questioner, but not giving a straight answer, (3) a request by the followers for elucidation after the opponent's departure, (4) and a private explanation to them in clear language.[20] Several difficulties are left unresolved with this explanation. It is not certain that a form known from rabbinical literature was familiar to the composer of the Gospel. Nor is there any evidence of opponents to Jesus in this particular passage. Finally, it still does not resolve the disturbing image of Jesus declaring that some are destined to be on the "outside."

Another approach is to reexamine the translation of Mark 4:10-12. Joachim Jeremias proposes that an Aramaic substratum (Jesus' original language) underlies the text of the Greek New Testament and that the Aramaic word *dil^ema* has been misunderstood. Accordingly, the last part of v. 12 should read, *"unless* they turn and God will forgive them."[21] Jeremias bases his reconstruction on parallels between Mark 4:12 and the translation of Isaiah 6:10 in the Aramaic Targum of Isaiah. This is problematic because the extant text of the Targum dates only to the fourth or fifth century C.E.

Other commentators have interpreted these verses as a composition of the early church, who explained Israel's lack of acceptance of Jesus as having been God's predetermined plan. Similar sayings can be found in Romans 9:16-29; 10:16-21; 11:7-10; John 12:37-41; Acts 28:25-28.[22] This explanation is problematic for Mark's Gospel because of 12:12, where Jesus' Jewish

---

[19] See especially Mary Ann Beavis, *Mark's Audience. The Literary and Social Setting of Mark 4.11-12* (JSNTSup 33; Sheffield, JSOT Press, 1989).

[20] David Daube, *The New Testament and Rabbinic Judaism* (New York: Arno Press, 1973) 141–43; Stock, *Mark*, 144.

[21] Jeremias, *Parables*, 17.

[22] Donahue, *Parables*, 41.

opponents understand the parable perfectly well as spoken against them.

Many commentators[23] relate "the mystery of the kingdom of God" (v. 11) to the theory of the "messianic secret" first proposed at the turn of the century by William Wrede.[24] The theme that runs throughout the Gospel of Mark is that Jesus does not want his identity to be known. He forbids demons, unclean spirits, and people he heals to announce who he is (Mark 1:24-25, 34, 44; 3:11-12). In 8:27-30, after Peter declares Jesus as Messiah, Jesus warns the disciples not to tell anyone about him. Wrede's hypothesis was that these were not words of the historical Jesus, but a theme created by the evangelist for literary suspense and for theological reasons. Only when one reached the conclusion of the story could one properly understand the paradox of a crucified and risen Messiah.

With his theme of the messianic secret Mark was also indicating the discontinuity between the periods before and after the resurrection. Only in the post-paschal church did Jesus' identity and his message about the reign of God become clear to his followers. In the Gospel narrative this is signaled by the literary fiction created by Mark, whereby even after the mystery has been revealed to the disciples (4:11) they still do not understand (4:35-41; 6:45-52; 8:17-21) and they continue to need private instruction (7:17-22; 9:28-29; 10:10-12; 13:3-37).

Thus, the "mystery of the reign of God" entrusted to those who place themselves around Jesus (v. 11) is not something that remains incomprehensible (this is reaffirmed in 4:22) but is the paradoxical plan of God, now being revealed in Jesus, that salvation comes through one who is rejected and crucified.[25] To those who choose to remain with Jesus the meaning of the mystery will be gradually unfolded (v. 11). But those who choose to remain on the outside, have deliberately closed their eyes and ears so that they may not be converted (v. 12). Like the prophet Isaiah, Jesus' words have a mixed reception.

---

[23] E.g., Lambrecht, *Once More Astonished*, 105–07.

[24] William Wrede, *Das Messiasgeheimnis in den Evangelien* (Göttingen: Vandenhoeck & Ruprecht, 1901). The English translation, *The Messianic Secret* (London: James Clarke) appeared only in 1971.

[25] Donahue, *Gospel in Parable*, 42–46.

Jesus does not speak in parables so that some will not understand; their incomprehension is the result of their choice not to join those who struggle to follow.

THE PARABLE OF THE SOIL (vv. 13-20)

Most scholars believe that the explanation of the parable in vv. 13-20 is a secondary interpretation by the early Church.[26] With the exception of the weeds in the field (Matt 13:24-30, 36-43), no other Gospel parable has an allegorical explanation. It is more likely that Jesus left his stories with open-ended challenges. A linguistic analysis shows this to be the only instance in the Gospels of the absolute use of *ho logos*, "the word," a technical term for "the gospel" that occurs often in the Pauline letters and in Acts.[27] Also, the parallel in *Gos.Thom.* §9 does not have the interpretation, a sign that at one time the parable circulated without it. Moreover, the interpretation misses the eschatological point of the parable; it becomes, instead, an exhortation to self-examination.[28]

Nonetheless, these verses offer an important insight into how the early Church preached this parable of Jesus, and they give one direction for how it might yet be preached. The audience for vv. 13-20 remains "those present along with the Twelve" (v. 10). Jesus' question in v. 13 makes it imperative for them to understand this parable if they are to comprehend any of them.

The allegorical explanation in vv. 13-20 clearly focuses on the varying levels of receptivity of the four different types of soil, that is, four types of hearers of the word.[29] The kinds of

---

[26] For arguments for this position see Jeremias, *Parables*, 77–79; Donahue, *The Gospel in Parable*, 46–47. Michael P. Knowles ("Abram and the Birds in *Jubilees* 11: A Subtext for the Parable of the Sower?" *NTS* 41 [1995] 145–51) argues on source-critical grounds for an organic link between the parable and its interpretation in light of parallels with a story in *Jubilees* 11. David Flusser (*Die rabbinischen Gleichnisse und der Gleichniserzähler Jesus* 1. Teil: *Das Wesen der Gleichnisse* [Bern: Peter Lang, 1981] 20, 63, 119–20) also holds that interpretations of parables are not later additions but belong to the original accounts by Jesus.

[27] E.g., 2 Corinthians 11:4; 1 Thessalonians 1:6; 2:13; 2 Thessalonians 1:6; 2 Timothy 1:8; 2:9; Colossians 1:6, 10; Acts 6:7; 12:24; 17:11; 19:20.

[28] Jeremias, *The Parables of Jesus*, 28.

[29] Joel Marcus ("Blanks and Gaps in the Markan Parable of the Sower," *BibInt* 5 [1997] 247–62) points out that the one element that is not explained in

obstacles that a farmer would face from birds, rocks, thorns, and overexposure of seedlings to sun, are likened to stumbling blocks one faces, once having received the word. Deficient understanding, the work of the evil one, lack of rootedness in oneself, tribulation and persecution on account of the word, worldly concerns, and the lure of riches, all stand in the way of God's word[30] taking deep root and bearing fruit.[31]

From this vantage point the emphasis is on the hearer; each is exhorted to cull out all impediments and become "good soil." The parable not only explains why some hearers of the word "bear fruit" and others don't, but it calls those who hear to cultivate themselves for maximum receptivity and understanding.[32] For Mark's community it offers an explanation for why some have apostasized or abandoned the faith and why some are determined opponents of the Gospel from their first hearing of it.[33]

---

the allegorical interpretation is the identity of the sower. Is it God? Christ? the Christian preacher? Marcus proposes that this "gap" in the narrative allows for an identity of the Christian with God and Christ when preaching the word (similar to Mark 13:11).

[30] Some scholars have advanced that the "seed" in 4:15 can represent not only the "word" but also the people who hear the word and who are destined for the eschatological reign of God. They call on Hosea 2:25; Jeremiah 31:27 and 4 *Ezra* 8:41 for scriptural background for the double duty metaphor of seed as people. See Heil, "Reader Response," 278; L. Ramoroson, "'Parole-semence' ou 'Peuple-semence' dans la parabole du Semeur?" *ScEsp* 40 (1988) 91–101.

[31] There is a similar passage in the Mishnah that speaks of four different kinds of hearers as: those who are slow to hear and swift to lose; those who are slow to hear and slow to lose; those who are swift to hear and slow to lose; and those who are swift to hear and swift to lose (*m. ʾAbot* 5.10-15).

[32] Narrative analysis suggests that the elements in the parable of the sower are already illustrated by diverse character groups that have already appeared in the Gospel: The Pharisees are the seed that fell along the path; the disciples are the seed that fell on rocky ground; the crowds, prefigured by Herod, are the seed that fell among thorns; and the chief priests, scribes, and elders are the thorns that choke the word (Terence J. Keegan, "The Parable of the Sower and Mark's Jewish Leaders," *CBQ* 56 [1994] 511–12).

[33] Marcus, *Mystery*, 94.

PREACHING POSSIBILITIES

The task of the preacher is to discern which of the many possible points, the four outlined above, or others still, conveys the message that their congregation needs to hear at this time and place. Does the community struggle with inclusivity? Then the preacher would do well to focus on the Sower's profligate and indiscriminate sowing of the word. Is there discouragement over lack of results from efforts toward evangelization and justice? Then the parable could provide a word of encouragement about the assured efficacy of the seed, the word, and the bountiful harvest at the end time. Are there people in the congregation who are caught in impossible webs of oppression? Then the revolutionary image of an out-of-bounds harvest can give hope to an overturning of systems of domination.

Is the assembly growing lax in their efforts to cultivate themselves as receptive "soil" for the word? Then an exhortation to clear away the "rocks" and "thorns" and all other obstacles would be in order. In Mark's Gospel the disciples are fallible followers; they constantly struggle to understand. Mark 4:1-20 gives assurance about the mystery being revealed to disciples in the crucified Christ. But it also warns disciples that they can become outsiders;[34] more is required than an initial decision to follow Jesus.

LECTIONARY CONTEXT

In the weekday lectionary both the first reading and the Gospel reading are arranged semi-continuously. One would be hard pressed to make cogent connections between them. The preacher would do well to choose to preach on one of the readings rather than force a link.

In Year I the first reading is from Hebrews 10:11-18. Its subject is the perfect offering made by Jesus, the great high priest. This theme is picked up by the responsorial psalm (110:1-4), "You are a priest forever in the line of Melchisedek."

---

[34] G. Fay, "Introduction to Incomprehension: The Literary Structure of Mark 4:1-34," *CBQ* 51 (1989) 65–81.

In Year II the first reading is from 2 Samuel 7:4-17, concerning David's desire to build a permanent dwelling place for the Lord. The responsorial psalm, "Forever I will keep my love for him" (Ps 89:4-5, 27-28, 29-30) echoes Nathan's response to David in the first reading, where the prophet reaffirms God's covenant fidelity and the promise of an enduring throne to David.

CHAPTER TEN

Hidden and Revealed Light
(Mark 4:21-25)

Thursday, of the Third Week of Ordinary Time

Jesus said to the crowds:
"Is a lamp brought in to be placed under a bushel basket
or under a bed,
and not to be placed on a lampstand?
For there is nothing hidden except to be made visible;
nothing is secret except to come to light.
Anyone who has ears to hear ought to hear."
He also told them, "Take care what you hear.
The measure with which you measure will be measured out to you,
and still more will be given to you.
To the one who has, more will be given;
from the one who has not, even what he has will be taken away."

MARCAN LITERARY CONTEXT

Some commentators see these verses as the center of the whole parables discourse in Mark 4.[1] These independent sayings[2] are linked verbally and thematically to the parables that come before and after. Hidden things made manifest (v. 22) links with 4:10-12, 27, 34. Hearing (vv. 23, 24) framed the opening parable of the chapter (vv. 3, 9) and reappears in the concluding

[1] See above, chap. 6.

[2] Matthew scatters these four sayings in different contexts (5:15; 10:26; 7:2; 6:33b; 25:29), giving them different nuances from Mark. Luke uses some of these sayings twice. He scatters them in 11:33; 12:2; 6:38; 12:31b; 19:26. Some he repeats and places together (8:16-18) like Mark, after the explanation of the parable of the seed. Two versions of the saying about hidden things being revealed are found in *Gos.Thom.* §5 and §6; the logion about placing a lamp on a stand is in *Gos.Thom.* §33.

verses (v. 33). The audience for these sayings is the same as the preceding section: "those present along with the Twelve" (4:10) who question Jesus about the meaning of the parables after hearing his first one. The first two verses (4:21-22) are positive exhortation. The tone in vv. 23-25 shifts to a warning.

THE LAMP THAT COMES (4:21-22)

The opening question in v. 21 at first seems straightforward, drawing from common wisdom: one doesn't put a light under a bushel basket or under a bed, does one? The question is introduced with *mēti*, which presumes a negative answer, "Of course not." Closer examination of the wording reveals a peculiarity in v. 21.[3] The query is, literally, "a lamp doesn't *come in (erchetai)* to be put under a bushel, does it?" Matthew (5:15) and Luke (8:16) convert it to a statement and use a more expected phrase, "No one who lights[4] a lamp" (Luke 8:16). In view of the number of times that Mark uses the verb *erchomai*, "to come," of Jesus,[5] it is likely that he intends a christological nuance in 4:21.

If the light in v. 21 is meant to refer to Jesus, then the second verse is assuring the disciples that what is not understandable about him and his teaching will eventually come clear.[6] It reinforces what is said in 4:11 and 4:33-34, that the mystery of the reign of God is entrusted to disciples, and that it is in the process of coming to full revelation.

An alternative interpretation is that 4:21-23 be read as the concluding verses of the complex that begins in 4:1. Juxta-

---

[3] Donahue, *Gospel in Parable*, 48; Harrington, *Mark*, 60.

[4] Matthew uses the verb *kaiousin*, while Luke uses *hapsas*. The meaning ("lights") in this context is the same.

[5] Mark 1:14, 39; 6:1; 8:38; 10:45; 14:62. Donahue, *Gospel in Parable*, 48.

[6] Marcus, *Mystery*, 141–43 cites several passages in Jewish literature where a light or lamp can symbolize both a person and that person's teaching. Examples include Sirach 48:1, "Till like a fire there appeared the prophet whose words were as a flaming furnace;" 1QSb 4:27, "May God make of you . . . a great torch, a light to the world in knowledge, to enlighten the faces of many;" and *Sipre Num* 94:2-3, a commentary on Numbers 11:17: "What was Moses like in that hour? He was like a candle placed on a candlestick, from which many candles are lit, and its light is not lacking at all; thus Moses' wisdom was not lacking at all."

posed with verses 13-20, the explanation of the seed parable, verses 21-23 are meant to balance and clarify the interpretation (vv. 10-12)[7] that follows the parable proper (vv. 3-9). The parables should not be misconstrued as concealing (v. 21), rather, their function is to reveal. What is unveiled (v. 22) by the parables are the true loyalties of the hearers, and that is polarizing (vv. 10-12).[8] A slightly different variation on this interpretation is that vv. 21-22, when read in connection with vv. 11-12 imply that the secret given to the disciples must be proclaimed openly.[9] It was not meant to remain hidden. That it is being revealed at the moment to a closed circle is only temporary. The ultimate aim is proclamation to all.[10]

MEASURED HEARING (vv. 23-25)

Verse 23 repeats the phrase that comes at the conclusion of the parable of the sower (v. 9) and functions as a hinge, making the transition to vv. 24-25. The tone shifts to one of warning, but the substance of the warning is a matter of debate.

For some commentators the admonition in v. 24, "Take care what you hear," refers back to vv. 13-20. The care one gives to the soil will determine the measure of return.[11] Verse 25 can be understood to move toward eschatological judgment: the giving and taking refers to reward and punishment that is incurred after the time for action is past.[12]

From another perspective, one may question what is it that is given and taken away (vv. 24-25)? Is it special insight? This is the most common interpretation, partly because this seems to be how Matthew understands it (13:11-12). But perhaps

---

[7] Myers, *Binding the Strong Man*, 175–76; Fay, "Incomprehension," 72–73; Marcus, *Mystery*, 128–29.

[8] Myers, *Binding the Strong Man*, 175–76.

[9] Tuckett, "Mark's Concerns," 21.

[10] Lambrecht, *Once More Astonished*, 96.

[11] Matthew 7:2 and Luke 6:38 place the saying about measuring in a context of judgment, i.e., one will be judged in the measure in which one judges others. Mark's context gives the phrase a different meaning (Harrington, *Mark*, 60).

[12] Donahue, *Gospel in Parable*, 48.

v. 25 is a quotation of a popular proverb that states the obvious from a peasant point of view: the rich just keep getting richer, and the poor keep losing even the little they have.[13] This pessimistic saying about economic injustice is then denounced in the subsequent parables (vv. 26-29), which assure the listener that God's judgment on the ruling powers will come (from the allusion to Joel 3:13 in Mark 4:29). Revolutionary hope is held out to those who are resigned to thinking that nothing will ever change.

PREACHING POSSIBILITIES

If the first pair of sayings is christological in orientation, then the expression about what is hidden being brought to light is not one that is meant to strike fear in a person that their secret sins will be broadcast in daylight. Rather, it gives comfort to disciples that what they do not understand about the mysterious ways of God manifest in a crucified Messiah will be made clear. Or, if the parable is taken as a warning, it asserts that parables are polarizing stories. It admonishes that by one's response to the parables one's true loyalties are revealed.

Another slant on the theme of what is hidden being made clear is that disciples continue to learn throughout their lives. One never fully understands the mystery. If hearers have become cocky about their "insider" status, the parable can offer a humbling message that they still stand in a measure of unknowing while the mystery continues to be disclosed.

In a congregation that has become complacent about their efforts at evangelization, the parable can serve as a clarion to proclaim the word openly. Just as it is absurd to hide a lamp under a bushel basket or a bed, so is it unthinkable that disciples keep the word to themselves. Moreover, the benefit one receives in return will be in accord with the measure of self-extension in mission.

For those who live in oppressive circumstances the parable can shatter hopeless resignation that nothing can ever change. Looking ahead to a different kind of harvest (v. 29) it

---

[13] Jeremias, *Parables*, 62; Myers, *Binding the Strong Man*, 178–79.

can point toward God's ability to upend the present economic arrangement.

LECTIONARY CONTEXT

In Year I the first reading is from Hebrews 10:19-25. It gives Christians assurance of access to God by the means opened up by Christ. It further exhorts believers to rouse one another to love and good deeds and to gather with one another to pray in the assembly. The psalm response (24:1-2, 3-4, 5-6) comes from a processional hymn that may have been used as a reenactment of David's bringing the ark of the covenant to the Temple.[14] The first stanza proclaims God's ownership of all creation. The second and third acclaim that those who are sinless may come before God and receive blessing and reward. The responsorial verse, "Lord, this is the people that longs to see your face," expresses the desire of the worshiper to stay always in God's presence.

In Year II the first reading is 2 Samuel 7:18-19, 24-29, where David reminds God of the assurance made to him that his "house" of descendants would endure forever. David entreats God to fulfill this generous promise. The responsorial psalm (132:1-2, 3-5, 11, 12, 13-14) reiterates the promise, and reminds David's offspring of the necessity to keep the covenant decrees.

Since both the first reading and the Gospel reading are arranged semi-continuously in the weekday lectionary, connections between them are not readily apparent. The preacher would do well to choose to preach on one of the readings rather than force an artificial connection.

---

14 Nowell, *Sing a New Song*, 232.

CHAPTER ELEVEN

Murderous Tenants and Rejected Stone
(Mark 12:1-12)

Monday of the Ninth Week of Ordinary Time

[Jesus] began to speak to [the chief priests, the scribes,
*   and the elders] in parables.*
"A man planted a vineyard, put a hedge around it,
*   dug a wine press, and built a tower.*
Then he leased it to tenant farmers and left on a journey.
At the proper time he sent a servant to the tenants
*   to obtain from them some of the produce of the vineyard.*
But they seized him, beat him,
*   and sent him away empty-handed.*
Again he sent them another servant.
And that one they beat over the head and treated shamefully.
He sent yet another whom they killed.
So, too, many others; some they beat, others they killed.
He had one other to send, a beloved son.
He sent him to them last of all, thinking, 'They will respect my son.'
But those tenants said to one another, 'This is the heir.
Come, let us kill him, and the inheritance will be ours.'
So they seized him and killed him,
*   and threw him out of the vineyard.*
What [then] will the owner of the vineyard do?
He will come, put the tenants to death,
*   and give the vineyard to others.*
Have you not read this scripture passage:

> *'The stone that the builders rejected*
> *   has become the cornerstone;*
> *by the Lord has this been done,*
> *   and it is wonderful in our eyes'?"*

They were seeking to arrest him, but they feared the crowd,
for they realized that he had addressed the parable to them.
So they left him and went away.

MARCAN LITERARY CONTEXT

The parable of the tenants is situated in Jesus' brief ministry in Jerusalem. Conflict with the chief priests, scribes, and elders over his authority has already set the stage (11:27-33). In the episodes that follow the Jerusalem leaders continue to challenge Jesus on questions of paying tax to the emperor, belief in the resurrection, the greatest commandment, and Davidic sonship (12:13-37). The parable can be seen as the centerpiece of this section of the Gospel:[1]

11:1-11   Jesus arrives in the Temple and observes the scene
11:12-33   Discussion about Jesus' appearance in the Temple
12:1-12   The parable of the murderous winegrowers
12:13-40   Discussions about a number of issues
12:41–13:2   Jesus observes the people in the Temple and leaves.

As the hinge piece between Jesus' cursing of the fig tree, symbolizing destruction of the Temple (11:12-25), and his prophetic pronouncement of the dismantling of the temple (13:2), the parable focuses attention on those entrusted with Temple leadership. Jesus addresses the parable to the chief priests, the scribes, and the elders (11:27, the referent for the pronoun "them" in 12:1). Unlike the parables in Mark 4 and 7 that require explanation from Jesus, this one is understood clearly by the Jerusalem leaders and intensifies their resolve to do away with Jesus (12:12). Their murderous intentions have already been articulated in 3:6 and 11:18. They delay arresting Jesus, however, for fear of the crowd, who up to this point has been favorable toward him.[2]

---

[1] Bas van Iersel, *Reading Mark*, 42. Joanna Dewey, *Markan Public Debate*, 152–67, likewise sees 11:11 and 13:2 as a frame around Jesus' public Jerusalem ministry. She advances that 12:1-12 plays a double role. It forms a rhetorical subunit with 11:15-18 and 11:27-33 to make an extended controversy-objection-vindication pattern. It also introduces a symmetrical complex of debates in 12:1-40.

[2] The crowd plays a favorable role in Mark beginning with 2:4 where they surround him at the healing of the man who had been paralyzed. Throughout

PROVENANCE OF THE PARABLE

There are actually two parables in Mark 12:1-12. The first (vv. 1-9) deals with the murderous tenants; the second (vv. 10-12) introduces the rejected stone. In the present arrangement each part provides an interpretive clue to the other. But many scholars question whether the two were always joined and whether or not they came from the lips of Jesus. Many think that the allegorical nature of the passage and its narratively illogical elements point to its composition by the early Church, rather than being a parable told by Jesus.[3] Others think that only vv. 10-12 are secondarily appended. Still others argue for the integrity of the passage from its earliest composition.[4] We will treat the text as a whole as it presently stands.[5]

---

the Gospel they continue to flock to him for teaching and healing and respond to him positively (3:32-34). Only at 14:43 do they become hostile to Jesus. There the crowd has been sent by the chief priests, scribes, and elders as part of the retinue that arrests Jesus. In 15:8, 11, 15 the crowd, again incited by the chief priests, asks for the release of Barabbas in place of Jesus.

[3] For different analyses of the tradition history see Klyne Snodgrass, *The Parable of the Wicked Tenants* (Tübingen: Mohr [Siebeck], 1983) 41–71 and John Dominic Crossan, "The Parable of the Wicked Husbandmen," *JBL* 90 (1971) 451–65. Snodgrass argues that Matthew's version is the earliest account because it is more understandable as a story and most easily explains the shape of the other two. He finds no reason to doubt that the parable originated with Jesus. Crossan believes that in this particular instance the parallel in *Gos.Thom.* §65 represents an independent tradition that is more original than the Synoptic versions. The version in *Gos.Thom.* is more authentically parabolic in form; in the Synoptic Gospels it has become an allegory. Johannes C. DeMoor ("The Targumic Background of Mark 12:1-12: The Parable of the Wicked Tenants," *JSJ* 29 [1998] 63–80) argues for a Jewish origin of the parable on the basis of parallels in Targumic literature for each of its details. While the Targums date later than the New Testament, DeMoor advances that the metaphors employed in targumic exegesis would have been familiar to a pre-70 C.E. audience.

[4] Snodgrass, *Wicked Tenants*, 63–65, 97, 113–18, argues that the quotation from Psalm 118 should not be separated from the parable. A link between the two parts is forged by a word-play between בן, "son," and אבן, "stone," in the original Aramaic form of the parable. Moreover, rabbinic parables often end with a Scripture citation. David Flusser (*Die rabbinischen Gleichnisse und der Gleichniserzähler Jesus* 1. Teil: *Das Wesen der Gleichnisse* [Bern: Peter Lang, 1981] 20, 63, 119–20) argues similarly: that interpretations of parables are not later additions but belong to the original accounts by Jesus.

[5] For the most recent overview of current research on the parable see

The story reflects well the situation of unrest that existed in Galilee at the time of Jesus and continued to intensify up to the first Jewish revolt against Rome (66–70 c.e.). The economic situation for many was desperate. Famine, lack of rain, over-population, and heavy taxes could put a struggling farmer over the brink. In Palestine of Jesus' day it is estimated that somewhere between one-half and two-thirds of a farmer's income went to taxes that included Roman tribute, payment to Herod and the procurators, and land rent to the large landowners. Land remained all important. A peasant would go to any length to retain or regain its ownership. The murderous hostility of the laborers toward an absentee landlord is a true-to-life detail for first-century Palestine.[6]

A FAMILIAR STORY WITH A NEW ENDING

As the story begins, the allusion to Isaiah 5 is unmistakable and may be the key to the interpretation of Mark's parable.[7] Both texts relate the same actions of the vinegrower: he plants, digs a winepress, and builds a tower (Isa 5:1-2; Mark 12:1). There is the same narrative buildup to the climactic expectation of enjoyment of the produce and the same disappointment that such does not materialize. The same question is posed by the owner: What will he do? (Isa 5:4; Mark 12:9). Setting forth a question to the hearers is good parabolic technique that engages the listener and demands a decision. As such, Mark 12:9a may have been the original ending of the parable.[8]

Klyne R. Snodgrass, "Recent Research on the Parable of the Wicked Tenants: An Assessment," *BullBibRes* 8 (1998) 187–216.

[6] Oakman, *Economic Questions*, 57–72; Dodd, *Parables*, 94; Snodgrass, *Wicked Tenants*, 31–40.

[7] Similar references to Israel as a vineyard planted by God are found in Jeremiah 2:21; Hosea 10:1.

[8] The parallel parable in *Gos. Thom.* §65 ends with the death of the son and the enhortation, "Whoever has ears should hear." Jeremias (*Parables*, 70–77) argues that if the parable was a composition of the early Church they would not have concluded it here with the death of the son and no reference to the resurrection. Jeremias believes the parable comes from Jesus, with the allegorical elements added later. The quotation from Psalm 118 was appended when the

But as Mark 12:1-12 now stands, there is a critical difference in its ending as compared to that of Isaiah 5. In the latter
the vinegrower is clearly YHWH who is disappointed with the
yield of sour grapes from his carefully cultivated vine, Israel
(Isa 5:7). God announces its fate: "Take away its hedge, give it
to grazing, / break through its wall, let it be trampled! / Yes, I
will make it a ruin: / it shall not be pruned or hoed, / but
overgrown with thorns and briers; / I will command the
clouds / not to send rain upon it" (Isa 5:5-6). Mark, however,
does not simply repeat the familiar story. He offers a new version in which not the vineyard but the tenants are destroyed
(v. 9b). The vineyard remains and is entrusted to others. Israel
is still capable of producing a good harvest. It is the unrespon-
sive Temple leaders who will be replaced.[9]

The parable does not specify who are the "others" to whom
the vineyard will be entrusted. It is clear from v. 12 that the
current "tenants" are the Jerusalem authorities who oppose
Jesus. In vv. 10-11 the quotation of Psalm 118 advances the
point of the parable and functions like Nathan's accusation
"You are the man!" in his parable to David (2 Sam 12:7).[10] Only
at this point is it clear that the parable is directed at the abusive
religious authorities. Psalm 118 recalls God's unlikely choice
of David as king and messianic prototype. This allusion points
toward the new leadership of Israel as coming from those currently rejected as unimportant. Mark's readers may well have
understood this to mean the followers of the rejected Jesus.[11]

THE ENVOYS

An aspect of Mark's story that does not have a parallel in
Isaiah is the owner's repeated sending of servants and finally

---

parable was allegorically applied to Christ. It supplied scriptural grounds for
the fate of Jesus as the son and pointed toward his resurrection. Acts 4:11 and 1
Peter 2:7 also interpret Psalm 118 as pointing toward the risen Christ. Snodgrass, *Wicked Tenants*, 64–65, disagrees. The quotation is too indirect to be a
proof text added by the early Church.

[9] Aaron Milavec, "The Identity of 'the Son' and 'the Others': Mark's Parable of the Wicked Husbandmen Reconsidered," *BTB* 20 (1990) 34–35.

[10] Snodgrass, *Wicked Tenants*, 97.

[11] Milavec, "Identity," 35–37.

his son. A biblically attuned listener would hear resonances with God's persistent sending of prophet after prophet, habitually called "servants" (e.g., Jer 7:25; 25:4; Amos 3:7; Zech 1:6), many of whom suffered maltreatment and even death.[12] Efforts to identify particular prophets with the details of Mark 12:2-5 falter.[13] The designation of the final messenger as *agapētos,* "beloved son," (v. 6) recalls Mark 1:11 and 9:7, where Jesus is so identified at his baptism and transfiguration.

The motivation for sending the servants and for the killing of the son raise questions about verisimilitude in the story. Why would a landowner repeatedly send single servants and then his own beloved son? Is he stupid? Why does he not send a whole retinue so that they can overpower the rebellious tenants? And why do the tenants think they will possess the land if they kill the son? Various solutions are offered. For some scholars the story is allegorical, so that these details have symbolic meaning in view of salvation history. As such it is not necessary for every detail to cohere logically.

INHERITING THE LAND

The detail of the tenants' expectation of ownership by killing the son may not be so far-fetched as it first seems. There were cases in which an inheritance not claimed within a specified period of time could be considered "ownerless" and open to the first claimant.[14] Such a scenario may be envisioned by the parable. Verse 6 implies that the son is the sole heir, with the wording, "he had one other" and the designation of the son as *agapētos,* "beloved."[15] The tenants may think the owner who "left on a journey" (v. 1) has died and that the arrival of

---

[12] Snodgrass, *Wicked Tenants,* 79, points out that while in the Hebrew Scriptures there are related the murders of only two prophets (2 Chron 24:20-21; Jer 26:20), the killing of prophets is a frequent New Testament theme: Matthew 23:31-32; Luke 13:34; Acts 7:52; Hebrews 11:36-38; 1 Thessalonians 2:15.

[13] For some the second servant who suffers a head-wound is meant to be the beheaded John the Baptist.

[14] Jeremias, *Parables,* 74–76.

[15] The LXX translates the Hebrew word יָחִיד, "only" as ἀγαπητός, "beloved," at Genesis 22:2, in reference to Isaac. The sense is that an only son is especially beloved.

the son means he has come to claim his inheritance. If they kill the sole heir, they can be the first to lay claim to the "owner-less" property. Another explanation is based on a rabbinic law that a person who lacked proper title deeds could sustain a claim to ownership if he could prove undisputed possession for three years.[16] There is also a certain narrative logic to the killing of the son. This detail heightens the viciousness of the tenants in the story so that the hearers clearly recognize their utter depravity and make a correct judgment regarding their fate.[17] Within Mark's narrative the parable parallels the dynamics of the Gospel plot. The murderous plans of the tenants in the vineyard match the sinister intent of the Temple authorities toward Jesus.[18]

PREACHING POSSIBILITIES

The traditional allegorical interpretation of this parable identifies the vineyard as Israel,[19] the tenants as Israel's rulers and leaders, the owner as God, the messengers as the proph-ets, the son as Christ, and the "others" to whom the vineyard has been entrusted as the Gentile church that "supplants" Is-rael.[20] There are currently a number of other possible interpre-tations offered by New Testament scholars.

One aspect of the traditional interpretation that should be firmly countered by preachers today is the idea that the Gentile

---

[16] Snodgrass, *Wicked Tenants*, 38, J. D. M. Derrett, *Law in the New Testament* (London: Darton, Longman & Todd, 1970) 289–306. William Herzog (*Parables as Subversive Speech* [Louisville: Westminster John Knox, 1994] 101–03) sketches a possible scenario in which the tenants were originally owners displaced by economic hardship. The owner attained the land through foreclosure on loans to free peasant farmers who were unable to pay off the loans because of poor harvests.

[17] Dodd, *Parables*, 97; Jeremias, *Parables*, 76.

[18] van Iersel, *Reading Mark*, 149. Scott, *Hear Then the Parable*, 253–54 pro-poses an allusion to Genesis 37:20 where the brothers of Joseph likewise say, "Come on, let us kill him." For Scott this allusion makes the parable question whether the kingdom will surely go to the promised heirs. Its frustrated end-ing queries whether the kingdom's true heirs will in the end triumph.

[19] Snodgrass, *Wicked Tenants*, 75, distinguishes that the vineyard in the parable does not stand for the nation of Israel, but rather the elect of God.

[20] E.g., Jeremias, *Parables*, 70.

church "supplants" the Jewish faith. Such a notion would be quite anachronistic on the lips of Jesus (if the parable is authentically his). Nor would such an interpretation fit the situation of Mark's community, for whom Christianity is still a movement within Judaism. The interpretation that the church "replaces" the Jews as God's people grew out of the historical conflicts between the early Christians their Jewish counterparts in the synagogue and from ongoing Christian efforts at self-definition. Such "replacement" or "supersessionist" theology continues to foment insidious anti-Judaism that is abhorrent in this post-Holocaust age. In its original telling the change of leadership envisioned in the parable is from Jewish leaders who oppose Jesus to Jews who follow him.[21] Just as early Christians may have heard a hope that those currently considered unimportant may eventually become the cornerstone of the new leadership, so the preacher today can encourage contemporary Christians who take unpopular minority positions on issues of justice.

It is possible that Jesus, foreseeing his own death,[22] told this parable to move his disciples to reflect in advance on how they would react when he would be put to death. If the original parable ended at v. 9a, the question "What [then] will the owner of the vineyard do?" leaves Jesus' followers to ponder their own course of action. One direction that the preacher might take with this question is to focus on the character of the vinegrower: what kind of person sends messenger after messenger including the only beloved son? The parable expresses Jesus' own experience of divine pathos and portrays God as one who is longing for a response. The choice faces the hearer: will you reject God's offer and incur self-condemnation? Or will you recognize God's invitation in the spurned keystone?[23]

If, as the narrative asserts, Jesus directed the parable to his opponents, he may have intended it not so much as a counterattack, as one last opportunity for them to recognize his true

---

[21] Jeremias, *Parables*, 76, interprets the parable as vindicating Jesus' offer of the good news to the poor.

[22] Dodd, *Parables*, 98; Snodgrass, *Wicked Tenants*, 102.

[23] Donahue, *Gospel in Parable*, 54–55.

identity and turn away from their murderous plans.[24] From this perspective the preacher may use the parable to speak about one's approach toward "enemies." Rather than respond to violence with violence, the pacific vinegrower keeps sending envoys in the hopes that the tenants will eventually accept them.[25] He does not give up on his opponents, but offers repeated opportunities for conversion. Of course, this interpretation depends on ending the parable at v. 9a—before the owner puts the tenants to death!

A different line of interpretation that also ends the parable at v. 9 strips the story of its allegorical elements and sees it as a true-to-life description of a peasant uprising against an oppressive landowner. From this perspective the owner in the parable is not God and the son is not Jesus. Rather, the parable depicts a typical peasant revolt and explores themes of land ownership and inheritance, forcing the hearers to examine their attitudes toward the use of violence. The parable portrays the futility of violence and demands the formulation of a different response to oppression.[26] This interpretation opens an opportunity for the preacher to explore non-violent, direct action responses to contemporary situations of exploitation and oppression.[27]

LECTIONARY CONTEXT

In Year I the first reading is from Tobit (1:1-2; 2:1-9), who is portrayed as a model Israelite even while in exile. He observes

[24] van Iersel, *Reading Mark*, 150–51.

[25] Milavec, "Identity," 32.

[26] Herzog, *Subversive Speech*, 98–113. Myers, *Binding The Strong Man*, 308–09, and James D. Hester, "Socio-Rhetorical Criticism and the Parable of the Tenants," *JSNT* 45 (1992) 27–57 take a similar approach. Malina and Rohrbaugh (*Social Science Commentary*, 255) suggest that if this parable at its earliest stage were not a counter-challenge by Jesus to his Jerusalem enemies, then it may have been a warning to landowners expropriating and exporting the produce of the land.

[27] Crossan, "Wicked Husbandmen," 451–65, takes the message in the opposite direction. He judges the form in *Gos.Thom.* §65 as closest to the original parable and interprets it as one that urges the hearer to recognize the opportunity in a crisis situation and act resolutely to accomplish their purpose. In its present form in Mark, the parable does not convey this message.

the Law by keeping the feast of Pentecost, the joyous celebration of the wheat harvest. Tobit's exemplary mercy toward his fellow sufferers is underscored by his willingness to let his festive meal be interrupted so as to perform a charitable deed.

The responsorial psalm (112:1-2, 3-4, 5-6), "Happy the one who fears the Lord," sings of genuine happiness that comes only from right relationship with God and other people.[28] Following the reading from Tobit, which ends with Tobit being mocked for his charitable deeds, the psalm promises that one who acts as he does will receive everlasting rewards: "his generosity shall endure forever" (v. 3). A loose connection can be made with the Gospel on the theme of inheritance. Verse 2 of the psalm assures that it is the descendants of the just who will be "mighty upon the land."

In Year II the first reading is from 2 Peter (1:2-7). It begins by reminding hearers of the gift from God that, when accepted, enables believers to live as sharers of the divine nature. It then moves to exhortation to live in such a way that one virtue builds upon another, culminating in love. The responsorial psalm (91:1-2, 14-15, 15-16) professes utter trust in God, in all circumstances. God, in turn, promises deliverance and salvation.

As is generally the case with the weekday lectionary, there is very little thematic connection among the readings. The preacher would do well to concentrate on only one of the assigned texts.

---

[28] Nowell, *Sing a New Song*, 252.

Conclusion

It is curious that while the Gospel of Mark has the fewest parables it has the most books and monographs devoted to exploring Marcan parable theory. Our aim has been not to give an exhaustive summary or analysis of all the work that has been done on the parables in Mark. Rather, our intent has been to sketch some of the new directions of Marcan parables research so as to aid the preacher in her or his understanding of the text. Our hope has been that this exploration of new possibilities of meaning will spark the creativity of preachers as they break open the word for their fellow believers. We have suggested ways in which the homilist may direct the parables, but ultimately the difficult task of discerning which is the word a particular congregation needs at this time and place rests with the preacher. While many points are possible and valid in parable interpretation, the effective homilist will do well to develop only one. Each time that a parable appears in the lectionary, the task of wrestling with the text begins again. There are no "one size fits all" interpretations.

In the Gospel of Mark the term parable applies to many varied kinds of figurative speech. Some are extended stories, others are wisdom sayings, still others are extended similes. Their function is varied. At times they comfort; at other times they instruct and exhort; at still others they challenge. They are directed to both insiders and outsiders. They invite outsiders in and warn insiders there is always a danger of finding oneself outside Jesus' circle. Discipleship involves more than a one-time assent. Christians continue to struggle as fallible followers without perfect understanding. They must wrestle not only with the parables, but with the entire gospel. Mark casts his whole Gospel as a parable: an open-ended story that is left for the hearer to complete. Let anyone who hears heed well.

Bibliography

Anderson, J. C. and S. D. Moore, eds. *Mark & Method. New Approaches in Biblical Studies.* Minneapolis: Fortress, 1992.

Aune, D., ed. *Greco-Roman Literature and the New Testament.* Atlanta: Scholars Press, 1988.

Bailey, R. ed., *Hermeneutics for Preaching. Approaches to Contemporary Interpretations of Scripture.* Nashville: Broadman, 1992.

Batey, R. A. "Jesus and the Theatre," *NTS* 30 (1984) 564–65.

Beasley-Murray, G. R. "The Parousia in Mark," *RevExp* 75 (1978) 565–81.

Beavis, M. A. *Mark's Audience. The Literary and Social Setting of Mark 4.11-12.* JSNTSup 33. Sheffield: JSOT Press, 1989.

Beck, R. R. *Nonviolent Story. Narrative Conflict Resolution in the Gospel of Mark.* Maryknoll, N.Y.: Orbis, 1996.

Best, E. *Following Jesus: Discipleship in the Gospel of Mark.* JSNTSup 4; Sheffield: JSOT Press, 1981.

Boff, C. and J. Pixley. *The Bible, the Church, and the Poor.* Theology and Liberation Series. Maryknoll, N.Y.: Orbis, 1989.

Botha, P. J. J. "The Historical Setting of Mark's Gospel: Problems and Possibilities," *JSNT* 51 (1993) 27–55.

Boucher, M. *The Mysterious Parable. A Literary Study.* CBQMS 6. Washington, D.C.: Catholic Biblical Association of America, 1977.

_____. *The Parables.* NTM 7. Wilmington, Del.: Glazier, 1981.

Bowker, J. W. "Mystery and Parable: Mark IV.1-20," *JTS* 25 (1974) 300–17.

Boys, M. "Parabolic Ways of Teaching," *BTB* 13 (1983) 82–89.

Blomberg, C. "Interpreting the Parables: Where Are We and Where Do We Go from Here?" *CBQ* 53 (1991) 50–78.

_____. *Interpreting the Parables.* Downers Grove, Ill.: InterVarsity Press, 1990.

Brown, S. "'The Secret of the Kingdom of God' (Mark 4:11)," *JBL* 92 (1973) 60–74.

Bultmann, R. *History of the Synoptic Tradition.* rev. ed.; New York: Harper & Row, 1968.

Cadoux, A. T. *The Parables of Jesus.* London: James Clarke, 1931.

Carlston, C. E. *The Parables of the Triple Tradition.* Philadelphia: Fortress, 1974.

Collins, A. Y., "The Apocalyptic Rhetoric of Mark 13 in Historical Context," *BR* 41 (1996) 5–36.

_____. *The Beginning of the Gospel. Probings of Mark in Context.* Minneapolis: Fortress, 1992.

Collins, R. "The Story of a Seed Growing by Itself. A Parable for our Times," *Emmanuel* 94 (1988) 446–52.

Cousar, C. B. "Eschatology and Mark's *Theologia Crucis.* A Critical Analysis of Mark 13," *Int* 24 (1970) 321–35.

Cranfield, C. E. B. *The Cambridge Greek Testament Commentary.* Cambridge: Cambridge University Press, 1959.

Crossan, J. D. *Cliffs of Fall. Paradox and Polyvalence in the Parables of Jesus.* New York: Crossroad, 1980.

_____. *The Dark Interval: Towards a Theology of Story.* Niles, Ill.: Argus, 1975.

_____. *In Parables: The Challenge of the Historical Jesus.* New York: Harper & Row, 1973.

_____. "The Parable of the Wicked Husbandmen," *JBL* 90 (1971) 451–65.

Culbertson, P. L. *A Word Fitly Spoken.* Albany: State University of New York Press, 1995.

Cuvillier, E. *Le concept de* ΠΑΡΑΒΟΛΗ *dans le second évangile.* EB n. s. 19. Paris: Gabalda, 1993.

Daube, D. *The New Testament and Rabbinic Judaism.* New York: Arno Press, 1973.

de Mello, A. *The Song of the Bird.* Garden City, NY: Doubleday, 1984.

DeMoor, J. C. "The Targumic Background of Mark 12:1-12: The Parable of the Wicked Tenants," *JSJ* 29 (1998) 63–80.

Derrett, J. D. M. *Law in the New Testament.* London: Darton, Longman & Todd, 1970.

Dewey, J. *Markan Public Debate. Literary Technique, Concentric Structure, and Theology in Mark 2:1–3:6.* SBLDS 48. Chico: Scholars Press, 1980.

_____. "The Literary Structure of the Controversy Stories in Mark 2, 1–3, 6," *JBL* 92 (1973) 394–401.

_____. "The Gospel of Mark," *Searching the Scriptures* Ed. E. Schüssler Fiorenza. New York: Crossroad, 1994. 2. 470–509.

Dodd, C. H. *The Parables of the Kingdom.* rev. ed. London: Collins, 1961.

Donahue, J. R. *The Gospel in Parable.* Philadelphia: Fortress, 1988.

_____. "A Neglected Factor in the Theology of Mark," *JBL* (1982) 563–94.

_____. "Aspects of New Testament Thought. The Parables of Jesus," *NJBC* 81.57–88, 1364–69.

_____. "Jesus as the Parable of God in the Gospel of Mark," *Int* 32 (1978) 369–86.

Doty, W. G. "An Interpretation: Parable of the Weeds and Wheat," *Int* 25 (1971) 185–93.

Drury, J. "The Sower, the Vineyard, and the Place of Allegory in the Interpretation of Mark's Parables," *JTS* 24 (1973) 367–79.

Dupont, J. "La parabole de la semence qui pousse toute seule (Marc 4,26-29)," *RSR* 55 (1979) 381–83.

Evans, C. A. "On the Isaianic Background of the Sower Parable," *CBQ* 47 (1985) 464–68.

_____. "A Note on the Function of Isaiah VI,9-10 in Mark IV," *RB* 88 (1981) 234–35.

Farmer, W. R. *The Synoptic Problem: A Critical Analysis.* New York: Macmillan, 1964.

Fay, G. "Introduction to Incomprehension: The Literary Structure of Mark 4:1-34," *CBQ* 51 (1989) 65–81.

Fitzmyer, J. A. "The New Testament Title 'Son of Man' Philologically Considered," in *A Wandering Aramean. Collected Aramaic Essays.* SBLMS 25; Chico, Calif.: Scholars Press, 1979. 143–60.

Flusser, D. *Die rabbinischen Gleichnisse und der Gleichniserzähler Jesus 1.* Teil: *Das Wesen der Gleichnisse.* Bern: Peter Lang, 1981.

Foley, E. *Preaching Basics.* Chicago: Liturgy Training Publications, 1998.

Freyne S. *Galilee from Alexander the Great to Hadrian 323 B.C.E. to 135 C.E.* University of Notre Dame Center for the Study of Judaism and Christianity in Antiquity 5. Wilmington, Del. and Notre Dame, Ind.: Glazier and University of Notre Dame Press, 1980.

Funk, R. W. *Language, Hermeneutics, and Word of God.* New York: Harper & Row, 1966.

_____. *Parables and Presence.* Philadelphia: Fortress, 1982.

_____. "The Looking-Glass Tree is for the Birds. Ezekiel 17:22-24; Mark 4:30-32," *Int* 27 (1973) 3–9.

Funk, R. W., B. B. Scott, & J. R. Butts. *The Parables of Jesus. Red Letter Edition. A Report of the Jesus Seminar.* Sonoma, Calif.: Polebridge, 1988.

Gerhardsson, B. "The Parable of the Sower and Its Interpretation," *NTS* 14 (1968) 165–93.

Goan, S. "To See or Not to See . . . Mark 4:10-12 Revisited," *MillStud* 25 (1990) 5–18.

Goulder, M. D. "Those Outside (Mk. 4:10-12)," *NovT* 33 (1991) 289–302.

Harrington, W. *Key to the Parables*. New York: Paulist, 1964.

_____. *Mark*. NTM 4. Wilmington, Del.: Glazier, 1979.

Hawkins, D. J. "The Incomprehension of the Disciples in the Markan Redaction," *JBL* 91 (1972) 491–500.

Heil, J. P. "Reader-Response and the Narrative Context of the Parables about Growing Seed in Mark 4:1-34," *CBQ* 54 (1992) 271–86.

_____. *The Gospel of Mark as a Model for Action. A Reader-Response Commentary*. New York: Paulist, 1992.

Hedrick, C. W. *Parables as Poetic Fictions*. Peabody: Hendrickson, 1994.

Hendrickx, H. *The Parables of Jesus*. rev. ed. San Francisco: Harper & Row, 1986.

Hengel, M. *Studies in the Gospel of Mark*. Philadelphia: Fortress, 1985.

Herzog, W. *Parables as Subversive Speech*. Louisville: Westminster/John Knox, 1994.

Hester, J. D. "Socio-Rhetorical Criticism and the Parable of the Tenants," *JSNT* 45 (1992) 27–57.

Hilkert, M. C. *Naming Grace. Preaching and the Sacramental Imagination*. New York: Continuum, 1997.

Hoppe, Leslie, "Parables. Stories with Double Meanings," *St. Anthony Messenger* (October, 1993) 24–27.

Jeremias, J. *The Parables of Jesus*. rev. ed. New York: Scribner's Sons, 1963.

_____. *Rediscovering the Parables of Jesus*. New York: Scribner's Sons, 1966.

Jones, P. R. "Preaching on the Parable Genre," *RevExp* 94 (1997) 231–45.

Kee, A. "The Old Coat and the New Wine, A Parable of Repentance," *NovT* 12 (1970) 13–21.

Kee, H. C. *Community of the New Age: Studies in Mark's Gospel*. Philadelphia: Westminster, 1977.

Keegan, T. J. "The Parable of the Sower and Mark's Jewish Leaders," *CBQ* 56 (1994) 501–18.

Kelber, W. *The Kingdom in Mark: A New Place and a New Time*. Philadelphia: Fortress, 1974.

_____. *The Oral and Written Gospel*. Philadelphia: Fortress, 1983.

Kirkland, J. R. "The Earliest Understanding of Jesus' Use of Parables: Mark IV,10-12 in Context," *NovT* 19 (1977) 1–21.

Knowles, J. K. "Abram and the Birds in *Jubilees* 11: A Subtext for the Parable of the Sower?" *NTS* 41 (1995) 145–51.

Krentz, E. *The Historical-Critical Method*. Guides to Biblical Scholarship. Philadelphia: Fortress, 1975.

LaVerdiere, E. "Teaching in Parables," *Emmanuel* 94 (1988) 438–45, 453.

Lambrecht, J. *Once More Astonished: The Parables of Jesus*. New York: Crossroad, 1981.

Linnemann, E. *Jesus of the Parables*. New York: Harper & Row, 1966.

Lührmann, D. "Die Pharisäer und die Schriftgelehrten im Markusevangelium," *ZNW* 78 (1987) 169–85.

Malbon, E. S. *Narrative Space and Mythic Meaning in Mark.* San Francisco: Harper & Row, 1986.

_____. "Fallible Followers: Women and Men in the Gospel of Mark," *Semeia* 28 (1983) 29–48.

_____. "The Jesus of Mark and the Sea of Galilee," *JBL* 103 (1984) 363–77.

_____. "The Jewish Leaders in the Gospel of Mark. A Literary Study of Marcan Characterization," *JBL* 108/2 (1989) 259–81.

_____. "Mark: Myth and Parable," *BTB* 16 (1986) 8–17.

Malina, B. J. and R. L. Rohrbaugh. *Social Science Commentary on the Synoptic Gospels.* Minneapolis: Fortress, 1992.

_____. *The New Testament World. Insights from Cultural Anthropology,* rev. ed. Louisville: Westminster John Knox, 1993.

Marcus, J. "Blanks and Gaps in the Markan Parable of the Sower," *BibInt* 5 (1997) 247–62.

_____. "Mark 4:10-12 and Marcan Epistemology," *JBL* 103 (1984) 447–74.

_____. *The Mystery of the Kingdom of God.* SBLDS 90 Atlanta: Scholars Press, 1986.

Marion, D. "Simples et mystérieuses paraboles. X. La parabole-mystère Marc 4, 1-34," *EspVie* 106 (1996) 273–82.

Marxsen, W. *Mark the Evangelist.* Nashville: Abingdon, 1969.

May, D. M. "Mark 3:20-35 from the Perspective of Shame/Honor," *BTB* 17 (1987) 83–87.

McArthur, H. K. "The Parable of the Mustard Seed," *CBQ* 33 (1971) 198–210.

McCowen, A. *Personal Mark. An Actor's Proclamation of St. Mark's Gospel.* New York: Crossroad, 1985.

McFague, S. *Models of God. Theology for an Ecological, Nuclear Age.* Philadelphia: Fortress, 1987.

_____. *Speaking in Parables: A Study in Metaphor and Theology.* Philadelphia: Fortress, 1975.

Mearns, C. L. "Parables, Secrecy and Eschatology in Mark's Gospel," *SJT* 44 (1991) 423–42.

Meier, J. P. *A Marginal Jew. Rethinking the Historical Jesus.* ABRL, vol. 1, New York: Doubleday, 1991.

Mesters, C. *Defenseless Flower. A New Reading of the Bible.* Maryknoll, N.Y.: Orbis, 1989.

Meyer, M. *The Gospel of Thomas.* HarperSanFrancisco, 1992.

Milavec, A. "The Identity of 'the Son' and 'the Others': Mark's Parable of the Wicked Husbandmen Reconsidered," *BTB* 20 (1990) 30–37.

Moloney, F. J. *The Gospel of the Lord. Reflections on the Gospel Readings. Year B.* Collegeville: The Liturgical Press, 1993.

Moore, W. E. "'Outside' and 'Inside': A Markan Motif," *ExpTim* 98 (1986) 39–43.

Mowery, R. "Pharisees and Scribes, Galilee and Jerusalem," *ZNW* 80 (1989) 266–68.

Muddiman, J. "Fast, Fasting," *ABD* 2.773–76.

Myers, C. *Binding the Strong Man. A Political Reading of Mark's Story of Jesus.* Maryknoll, N.Y.: Orbis, 1988.

Neirynck, F. *Duality in Mark. Contributions to the Study of the Markan Redaction.* Leuven: Leuven University Press, 1972.

Neusner J. *From Politics to Piety. The Emergence of Pharisaic Judaism.* Englewood Cliffs, N.J.: Prentice Hall, 1973.

Newell, J. E. and R. R. "The Parable of the Wicked Tenants," *NovT* 14 (1972) 226–37.

Neyrey, J. "The Idea of Purity in Mark's Gospel," *Semeia* 35 (1986) 91–128.

Nowell, I. *Sing a New Song. The Psalms in the Sunday Lectionary.* Collegeville: The Liturgical Press, 1993.

Oakman, D. *Jesus and the Economic Questions of His Day.* SBEC 8. Lewiston/Queenston: Mellen, 1986.

Osiek, C. "Literal Meaning and Allegory," *TBT* 29/5 (1991) 261–66.

_____. *What Are They Saying About the Social Setting of the New Testament?* 2d ed. New York: Paulist, 1992.

Parker, A. *Painfully Clear. The Parables of Jesus.* Biblical Seminar 37. Sheffield: Sheffield Academic Press, 1996.

Patte, D. *What Is Structural Exegesis?* Guides to Biblical Scholarship; Philadelphia: Fortress, 1976.

Patten, P. "The Form and Function of Parable in Select Apocalyptic Literature and their Significance for Parables in the Gospel of Mark," *NTS* 29 (1983) 246–58.

Pavur, C. N. "The Grain is Ripe: Parabolic Meaning in Mark 4:26-29," *BTB* 17 (1987) 21–23.

Perelmuter, H. G. *Siblings. Rabbinic Judaism and Early Christianity at their Beginnings.* New York: Paulist, 1989.

Perkins, P. *Hearing the Parables of Jesus.* New York: Paulist, 1981.

Perrin, N. *Jesus and the Language of the Kingdom.* Philadelphia: Fortress, 1976.

Pilch, J. J. *The Cultural World of Jesus. Sunday by Sunday, Cycle A.* Collegeville: The Liturgical Press, 1995.

_____. *The Cultural World of Jesus. Sunday by Sunday, Cycle B.* Collegeville: The Liturgical Press, 1996.

Powell, M. A. *What is Narrative Criticism?* Guides to Biblical Scholarship; Philadelphia: Fortress, 1990.

Praeder, S. M. *The Word in Women's Worlds. Four Parables.* Zacchaeus Studies: New Testament. Wilmington, Del.: Glazier, 1988.

Pryor, J. W. "Markan Parable Theology - an Inquiry into Mark's Principle of Redaction," *ExpTim* 83 (1972) 242–45.

Race, M. and L. Brink. *In This Place. Reflections on the Land of the Gospels for the Liturgical Cycles.* Collegeville: The Liturgical Press, 1998.

Ramaroson, L. "Jésus semeur de parole et de peuple en Mc 4,3-9 et par.," *ScEs* 47 (1995) 287–94.

Reid, B. E. "Once Upon a Time . . . Parable and Allegory in the Gospels," *TBT* 29/5 (1991) 267–72.

_____. "Parables: Stories that Can Turn Your World Upside Down," *Praying* 55 (1993) 21–24.

_____. "Preaching Justice Parabolically," *Emmanuel* 102/6 (1996) 342–47.

Reid, B. E. and L. J. Hoppe. *Preaching From the Scriptures. New Directions for Preparing Preachers.* Pulaski, Wis.: Franciscan Printing Press, 1998.

Rhoads, D. and D. Michie. *Mark As Story.* Philadelphia: Fortress, 1982.

Rohrbaugh, R. L. "A Peasant Reading of the Parable of the Talents/Pounds: A Text of Terror?" *BTB* 23 (1993) 32–39.

_____. "The Social Location of the Markan Audience," *Int* 47 (1993) 380–95.

Rowland, C. and M. Corner. *Liberating Exegesis. The Challenge of Liberation Theology to Biblical Studies.* Louisville: Westminster/John Knox, 1989.

Ruether, R. R. *Gaia and God.* HarperSanFrancisco, 1992.

Sabin, M. "Reading Mark 4 as Midrash," *JSNT* 45 (1992) 3–26.

Sabourin, L. "The Parables of the Kingdom," *BTB* 6 (1976) 115–60.

Saldarini, A. *Pharisees, Scribes and Sadducees in Palestinian Society.* Wilmington, Del.: Glazier, 1988.

Schuller, E. "The Bible in the Lectionary," *Catholic Study Bible.* Ed. Donald Senior. New York: Oxford, 1990. 440–51.

Schweizer, E. "From the New Testament Text to the Sermon. Mk. 4:1-20," *RevExp* 72 (1975) 181–88.

_____. *The Good News According to Mark.* Atlanta: John Knox, 1970.

Schüssler Fiorenza, E. *Jesus: Miriam's Child, Sophia's Prophet* (New York: Continuum, 1994).

Scott, B. B. *Hear Then the Parable.* Minneapolis: Fortress, 1989.

Segal, A. F. *Rebecca's Children*. Cambridge: Harvard University Press, 1987.

Sellew, P. "Oral and Written Sources in Mark 4.1-34," *NTS* 36 (1990) 234–67.

Siegfried, R. and E. Ruane, eds. *In the Company of Preachers*. Collegeville: The Liturgical Press, 1993.

Snodgrass, K. *The Parable of the Wicked Tenants*. WUNT 27. Tübingen: Mohr [Siebeck], 1983.

_____. "Recent Research on the Parable of the Wicked Tenants: An Assessment," *BullBibRes* 8 (1998) 187–216.

Standaert, B. *L'Évángile selon Marc*. Lire la Bible 61; Paris: Cerf, 1983.

_____. *L'Evangile selon Marc: Composition et genre littéraire*. Brugge: Sint Andriesabdij, 1978.

Stock, A. *The Method and Message of Mark*. Wilmington: Glazier, 1989.

_____. "Jesus, Hypocrites, and Herodians, *BTB* 16 (1986) 3–7.

Stuhlmueller, C., ed. *The Collegeville Pastoral Dictionary of Biblical Theology*. Collegeville: The Liturgical Press, 1996.

Sweetland, D. *Our Journey with Jesus: Discipleship According to Mark*. GNS 22; Wilmington, Del.: Glazier, 1987.

Talbert, C. H. "Once Again: Gospel Genre," *Semeia* 43 (1988) 53–73.

Tannehill, R. C. "The Disciples in Mark: The Function of a Narrative Role," *JR* 57 (1977) 386–405.

Telford, W. R. *The Barren Temple and the Withered Tree*. JSNTSup1. Sheffield: JSOT Press, 1980.

Telford, W. R., ed. *The Interpretation of Mark*. 2d ed. Edinburgh: T. & T. Clark, 1995.

Thoma, C. and M. Wyschogrod, eds., *Parable and Story in Judaism and Christianity*. New York: Paulist, 1989.

Tolbert, M. A., "How the Gospel of Mark Builds Character (Characterization in the Parable of the Sower)," *Int* 47 (1993) 347–57.

_____. "Mark," *The Women's Bible Commentary*. Ed. C. A. Newsom and S. H. Ringe. Louisville: Westminster John Knox, 1992. 350–62.

_____. *Perspectives on the Parables*. Philadelphia: Fortress, 1979.

Tuckett, C. M. "Mark's Concerns in the Parables Chapter (Mark 4, 1-34)," *Bib* 69 (1988) 1–26.

Tyson, J. B. "The Blindness of the Disciples in Mark," *JBL* 80 (1961) 261–68.

van Iersel, Bas. *Reading Mark*. Collegeville: Liturgical Press, 1986.

Via, D. O. *The Parables: Their Literary and Existential Dimension*. Philadelphia: Fortress, 1967.

Waznak, R. *An Introduction to the Homily*. Collegeville: The Liturgical Press, 1998.

Westermann, Claus. *The Parables of Jesus in the Light of the Old Testament.* Minneapolis: Fortress, 1990.

Wiesel, E. *The Gates of the Forest.* tr. Frances Frenaye. New York: Holt, Rinehart and Winston, 1966.

Wilder, A. *The Language of the Gospel.* New York: Harper & Row, 1964.

_____. *Jesus' Parables and the War of Myths.* Philadelphia: Fortress, 1982.

Williams, J. G. *Gospel Against Parable. Mark's Language of Mystery.* Bible and Literature 12; Sheffield: JSOT, 1985.

Winterhalter, R., with G. W. Fisk. *Jesus' Parables: Finding our God Within.* New York: Paulist, 1993.

Wrede, W. *The Messianic Secret.* London: James Clarke, 1971.

Young, B. H. *Jesus and His Jewish Parables. Rediscovering the Roots of Jesus' Teaching.* Theological Inquiries. New York: Paulist, 1989.

_____. *The Parables. Jewish Tradition and Christian Interpretation.* Peabody: Hendrickson, 1998.